968.11 P266b   F V
PARSON
BOTSWANA : LIBERAL DEMOCRACY
AND THE LABOR RESERVE IN SOUTH-
ERN AFRICA   26.00

BOTSWANA

PROFILES · NATIONS OF CONTEMPORARY AFRICA
Larry W. Bowman, Series Editor

Botswana: Liberal Democracy and the Labor Reserve in Southern Africa,
Jack Parson

Ethiopia: Transition and Development in the Horn of Africa,
Mullatu Wubneh and Yohannis Abate

Kenya: The Quest for Prosperity, Norman D. Miller

Mozambique: From Colonialism to Revolution, 1900–1982,
Allen Isaacman and Barbara Isaacman

Senegal: An African Nation Between Islam and the West, Sheldon Gellar

Tanzania: An African Experiment, Rodger Yeager

The Seychelles: Unquiet Islands, Marcus Franda

Swaziland: Tradition and Change in a Southern African Kingdom,
Alan Booth

The Comoro Islands: Struggle Against Dependency in the Indian Ocean,
Malyn Newitt

Cameroon, Mark W. Delancey

Ghana, Deborah Pellow and Naomi Chazan

Ivory Coast, Barbara C. Lewis

Nigeria, Timothy M. Shaw and Orobola Fasehun

Somalia, David D. Laitin and Said S. Samatar

Also of Interest

Nigeria in Search of a Stable Civil-Military System, J. 'Bayo Adekson

BOTSWANA

Liberal Democracy and the Labor Reserve in Southern Africa

Jack Parson

Westview Press • Boulder, Colorado

Gower • London, England

Profiles / Nations of Contemporary Africa

Jacket photo: Daniel Kwelagobe, Minister of Public Service and Information, holds a campaign rally in Molepolole, 1974. This photo, and all photos in this book, are by the author.

Published in 1984 in the United States of America by Westview Press, Inc., 5500 Central Avenue, Boulder, Colorado 80301; Frederick A. Praeger, Publisher

Published in 1984 in Great Britain by Gower Publishing Company Limited, Gower House, Croft Road, Aldershot, Hampshire GU11 3HR, England

Library of Congress Cataloging in Publication Data
Parson, Jack.
  Botswana: liberal democracy and the labor reserve
in southern Africa.
  (Profiles. Nations of Contemporary Africa)
  Bibliography: p.
  Includes index.
  1. Botswana—Politics and government. 2. Botswana—
Economic policy. 3. Botswana—Dependency on foreign
countries. I. Title. II. Series.
DT791.P37 1984   968.1′1   83-21723
ISBN 0-86531-297-4

British Library Cataloguing in Publication Data
Parson, Jack
  Botswana. (Africa profile)
  1. Botswana—History—1966–
  I. Title II. Series
968′1′103   DT791
ISBN 0-566-00714-2

Printed and bound in the United States of America

10   9   8   7   6   5   4   3   2   1

Contents

List of Illustrations vii

Preface ix

1   Botswana in Perspective 1

The Context 2
The Physical and the Social and Political Settings 4
Class, Politics, and Development in Botswana:
   A Political Economy Approach 13

**2   Colonialism, Underdevelopment, and Nationalism
in the Bechuanaland Protectorate** 15

The Precolonial Period to 1870 15
Colonialism and Underdevelopment in Bechuanaland:
   1870–1940 18
Nationalism in Bechuanaland: 1895–1966 26
Underdevelopment in Colonial Bechuanaland:
   A Summary 33

3   Political Evolution in Contemporary Botswana 35

Sociocultural Context 35
Institutional Change 38
Postcolonial Political Development 47

4   Development Strategy: Rationale 57

Political Economy of Botswana About 1966 57
Colonial Development: 1955–1966 60
Beginnings of a New Development Strategy: 1966–1970 61
Formulation of a Strategy: Principles and Specifics,
   1970–1980 62
Rationale of Development in Perspective 70

5   *Development Strategy: Implementation
     and Consequences* 72

     Administrative Capacity and Resource Generation 73
     Implementing Development Strategy: Resources and
          Their Investment 75
     Implementing Development Strategy: The Political
          Economy of Growth 86

6   *Botswana in the World:
     Diplomacy of a Frontline State* 101

     Bechuanaland/Botswana in a South African Orbit 101
     Institutionalizing International Relations 103
     Diversification of Dependence............................. 104
     On the Front Line: Botswana and Liberation in
          Southern Africa 106
     Botswana in the World Perspective 111

7   *Political Economy of Botswana: Yesterday,
     Today, and Tomorrow* 113

     Yesterday: The Labor Reserve in History.................. 113
     Today: Dependent Development............................ 114
     And Tomorrow? Problems of Dependent Development 116

Notes 119
Selected Bibliography 135
Index 139

Illustrations

Tables

3.1 National Assembly elections by year and party 48

5.1 Proportion of development expenditures financed from
external sources, 1966/1967–1980/1981 74

5.2 Domestic development expenditure 1973–1975 and
1976–1981 by major category 82

5.3 Domestic development expenditure 1979–1985
by major category 84

5.4 Urban working class and salariat wages per day,
1974–1980.. 93

Maps

1.1 Southern Africa... 2

1.2 Republic of Botswana 5

1.3 Natural vegetation in Botswana 7

Photographs

Serowe in the Central District................................. 10

Chief's *kgotla* and house in Molepolole........................ 17

Cattle in the Central District 24

1974 BDP poster picturing then-President Seretse Khama 32

Citizens of Botswana 36

A Botswana man 36

The National Assembly 39

A political rally in Molepolole, 1974 49

Tsholetsa House, headquarters of the Botswana
Democratic party 50

A polling place in Molepolole, 1974 53

South African labor recruiting compound 59

The main shopping mall in Gaborone 61

Mining the kimberlite pipe at Jwaneng 78

The main treatment plant at the Jwaneng diamond mine 79

Traditional housing in Serowe 85

Old and new intermingle in a house in Molepolole 85

The railway station and bus park in Gaborone 86

Trading stores in Mahalapye 97

A Botswana–South Africa border post 102

Preface

The Republic of Botswana is an exciting nation to write about—and study. For the student and scholar, it presents the problem of development in a small country that has a stark colonial history and is overshadowed by its powerful neighbor, South Africa; yet Botswana also represents a nearly unique instance of stability and growth, although that growth is internationally dependent and the resulting income is unequally distributed. For the informed public and policymakers, a book such as this one provides an introduction to the history of and changes in the social, political, and economic circumstances of an increasingly important African country. For these reasons, an analytical overview of Botswana is long overdue.

The origins of the book are to be found in research conducted over a five-year period (1973–1978) while I was a lecturer at what is now the University of Botswana. A collaborative effort with Dennis Cohen to produce teaching materials that are relevant to Botswana resulted in a coedited volume, *Politics and Society in Botswana* (Gaborone: University College of Botswana, 1976), and my dissatisfaction with the unevenness of secondary literature coverage and the absence of any thorough analysis led me to write a more comprehensive D.Phil. thesis, "The Political Economy of Botswana: A Case in the Study of Politics and Social Change in Post-Colonial Societies," at the University of Sussex (1979). The opportunity to write a book on Botswana for the Westview Nations of Contemporary Africa series provided the motivation to attempt a concrete and concise description and analysis. A grant from the College of Charleston in the summer of 1982 provided the resources to revisit Botswana, thus ensuring the timeliness of both the data and the interpretation of the implications of that data.

The perspective underlying the book is the result of changes in my view of the concept and reality of development because of experiences during a nine-year period of residence in Africa and one year in England. During four years in Uganda, research on the relationship between the emergence of African entrepreneurs and development led me to seriously question what is called "the modernization perspective." In Botswana, I began a continuing process of evolving what is called a political economy perspective that is rooted in Marx's insights into capitalist production.

This perspective provides the intellectual foundation for this book, but the analysis is not presented on a corresponding level of abstraction. Although concepts of class and state relations provide a consistent framework throughout the book, their definition and explication are developed in a concrete empirical analysis.

While in Botswana, I built up an enormous debt to a large number of people. At the university, I benefited greatly from an association with many colleagues, among whom were Dennis Cohen, Nelson Moyo, Thomas Tlou, Robson Silitshena, Charles Harvey, Marcus Balintulo, Fred Morton, Neil Parsons, and Martin Fransman. My students in Botswana were able research assistants as well as being a demanding audience for the results of my research activity. Many civil servants and elected officials very patiently aided the research effort, and I wish a full list of names could be given. My debt to those people is at least made public, and I am grateful for their patience and help.

At Sussex, I learned much from E. A. Brett, who more than anyone else ably guided the development of my theoretical orientation. At the Institute of Development Studies at Sussex, I learned a great deal from seminars given by and discussions with Charles Harvey, Michael Lipton, Michael Cowen, and Chris Colclough. Since returning to the United States, I have drawn on the work of or have had discussions with Joel Samoff, Robert Hitchcock, and Phil Morgan. Morgan, Ranwedzi Nengwekhulu, Robson Silitshena, and Fred Morton also commented on all or part of the manuscript.

Although the usual absolution from responsibility for the substance of this book applies to all the people mentioned, I cannot help but appreciate and acknowledge the collective nature of research and writing. This book is my responsibility alone, but a large number of people appear in its contours, however much in the shadows of my mind.

Larry Bowman's skillful editing greatly improved the coherence and readability of the manuscript. It has also been a real pleasure to work with Lynne Rienner and Deborah Lynes as well as others at Westview Press on this project; for their gentle handling of the manuscript and for the copy editing of Megan Schoeck I offer grateful thanks.

Finally, but most important, this book is dedicated to Nancy Nolte Parson, who shared in the lengthy experience that it incorporates. It is written for our children, Nia and Daniel, and the children of Botswana, in the certainty that the world they inherit will be different from my own and the hope that this effort to understand a part of my world will effect part of that change, perhaps for the better.

Jack Parson
Charleston, South Carolina

1

Botswana in Perspective

The Republic of Botswana is a small, landlocked southern African nation, and the elements of its domestic situation are similar to those of many recently independent African countries. Rapid growth in export-oriented extractive mining and cattle industries has generated an increasingly unequal distribution of assets, opportunities, and income, and these factors define the boundaries of sociopolitical class configurations and struggles. Yet Botswana has not yet suffered the political consequences that are typical of a growing juxtaposition of rich and poor. A multiparty, liberal-democratic electoral system produces local and national legislative and executive institutions that function according to the parliamentary model. Although one party, the Botswana Democratic party, has dominated the elections, it has not, when in power, resorted to systematic corruption, repression, or irregularities to achieve that result.

This situation is all the more remarkable given Botswana's regional and world position. The problems associated with being landlocked are compounded by Botswana's economic dependence on South Africa, its strong, potentially hostile southern neighbor. As in the past, Botswana's economic development is intimately connected with that of South Africa. Socially and politically, Botswana's nonracialism represents an area of sanity in comparison to South Africa's racial oppression. Because of these facts, there is a persistent element of fragility and vulnerability in Botswana that could be, but has not been, used to legitimate far more internal repression than exists. Beyond the region, Botswana is subject to world economic insecurity, uncertain markets, and the vagaries of superpower politics.

Although Botswana's size and resources are relatively inconsequential in world terms, the very fact that it exists under the previously outlined conditions makes it an important country. Understanding the problems and prospects, and opportunities and limits, of Botswana's development can yield insights into similar processes elsewhere in the third world as well as into the process of liberation in southern Africa itself.

1

MAP 1.1. Southern Africa.
Source: U.S. Department of State, Bureau of Public Affairs, "Background Notes: Botswana" (Washington, D.C., May 1983).

THE CONTEXT

Developing an understanding of Botswana can begin by looking at three broad contextual factors: the country's geopolitical position, its national economy in relation to the rest of southern Africa and the world, and its drive for growth and development.

The Geopolitical Position

Botswana is a territory of 220,000 square miles (570,000 square kilometers)—the size of France, Kenya, or the U.S. state of Texas—and is one of fourteen landlocked countries in Africa. Located in the center of southern Africa (see Map 1.1), it is bordered by South Africa on the east and south, Namibia on the west and north, and Zimbabwe on the northeast. In addition, it touches Zambia at one point along the Zambezi River.[1] Until Zimbabwe's independence in 1980, the border with Zambia was Botswana's only physical link with a majority-ruled state, and thus it was an important psychological link with the independent countries to the north.

Botswana's location creates problems of access to the outside world, which are compounded by the fact that the country depends on South Africa for trade and access. The bulk of Botswana's external trade goes through South Africa, as do most travelers to and from Botswana. The country's long borders with South Africa and South African–controlled Namibia are also a potentially serious security problem. With a population of less than 1 million, Botswana is in no position to ensure its national defense in the event of territorial incursions. If such incursions took place, they would most likely originate in South Africa because of Botswana's opposition to the continuation of the apartheid system in that country. Concern in Botswana over such incursions is quite real. In the words of the late president, Sir Seretse Khama: "It is very easy . . . to envisage a situation in which one of our neighbors might decide for whatever reason, real or imaginary, to deny us the use of her transportation facilities. Such a development would do untold harm to the economy of this country."[2] Or, as H.C.L. Hermans puts it: "To be land-locked is difficult enough. To be black and land-locked in southern Africa is a lonely and expensive experience."[3]

The Economic Context

The problems of Botswana's geopolitical position are complicated by its economic situation. Despite rapid growth since 1966, the economy is relatively poor, highly dependent, and mineral led. The gross domestic product (GDP) increased from 32.9 million pula (P) in 1965 to P 192 million in 1973/1974 and P 670.9 million in 1980.[4] Even taking inflation into consideration, real growth was substantial. However, GDP per capita was still low and unequally distributed. In 1973/1974, it was about P 293 and increased to P 716 in 1980.

Much of the growth was a result of the discovery and extraction of minerals, particularly diamonds. Diamond exports increased dramatically from a value of $5.3 million in 1971 to $32.1 million in 1975 to $182.9 million in 1979.[5] Total exports in 1979, worth $353.1 million, were dominated by minerals (69 percent) and meat (20 percent).

Imports of goods and services are an exceedingly important factor in the economy as a proportion of the food consumed has to be imported along with the bulk of manufactured goods and investment capital. In 1974/1975, for example, imports amounted to 69.7 percent of GDP, and they rose in 1980 to about 80 percent.[6]

Botswana's exports are marketed in a number of Western countries, but it receives the bulk of its imports from its southern neighbors. In 1974 and 1975, nearly two-thirds of all exports went to the United Kingdom and North America, and about three-quarters of all imports were from South Africa. In 1980, about 85 percent of the exports went to Europe and North America, and 87 percent of the imports came from South Africa.[7]

This "openness" of Botswana's economy is an indication that it is economically dependent, particularly on South Africa. Botswana is a member of the Southern African Customs Union, which is dominated by South Africa, and relies on imports of South African goods and the South African transportation system.[8] In addition, thousands of Batswana work on short-term contracts in South African mines, factories, and agriculture. One estimate put the number in 1979 at 36,174, or 8 percent of Botswana's labor force.[9]

Thus, Botswana's economic situation parallels its geopolitical one. It is vulnerable in both areas, and this vulnerability generates an outlook on and a context for growth and development. If nothing else, the geopolitical and economic contexts set boundaries or limits within which policy must be formulated.

The Drive for Growth and Development

Botswana's domestic and foreign policies are formed with a view to developing as rapidly as possible in a difficult environment and to at least committing the country to an equitable distribution of the GDP. Thus, rapid economic growth combined with rural development and "social justice" have been the objectives of planning in Botswana.[10] In addition, the country has sought to decrease its dependence on South Africa by diversifying its sources of expatriate manpower, private investment, and external financial aid. Furthermore, Botswana has played a leading role in regional development through its membership in the Frontline States and in the Southern African Development Coordination Conference.[11]

Put into practice, these efforts have not worked as well as it was hoped they would. There are still striking inequalities in the exercise of political power, access to means of production in agriculture, and the distribution of income, as well as a persistent need for employment in South Africa. In addition, the external environment places definite and irresolvable constraints on Botswana.

THE PHYSICAL AND
THE SOCIAL AND POLITICAL SETTINGS

The physical, social, and political settings of the country play important roles. The physical setting includes geography and climate as well as basic economic factors—infrastructure, agriculture, and mining. Factors in the social and political settings include human resources, employment and the standard of living, and the political structures as well as their interrelationships.

The Physical Setting

Geography and Climate. Botswana covers part of a large tableland and lies at an average altitude of approximately 3,300 feet (1,000 meters).[12] Its predominant feature is the Kalahari semi-Desert in the southeast— indeed, 84 percent of the country is covered by Kalahari sand, which supports thornbush savanna vegetation. The northwestern part of the country is dominated by the Okavango River and its delta (see Map 1.2), which actually reaches about 390 miles (628 kilometers) across northwestern Botswana from Zambia to Namibia. The delta is the terminus of a large catchment area, the origins of which are to the north in Angola. The northeastern part of Botswana is higher, and some tributaries of the Zambezi River cut across this area. The eastern section rises to a series of hills, which run north to south and are not covered by deep Kalahari sand.[13] It is in this area that arable farming is possible, grazing for cattle and goats is most available, and about 80 percent of the people live. About 4 percent of all the land can be easily cultivated; the bulk of the land, including much of the Kalahari Desert, is rangeland that is suitable for seasonal grazing.[14]

The primary physical problem—for man, crops, and animals—is the presence (or absence) of moisture—rainfall and permanent supplies of water. "Apart from the Okavango River system there is no permanent water in the Republic. On the eastern hilly fringes seasonal flow occurs

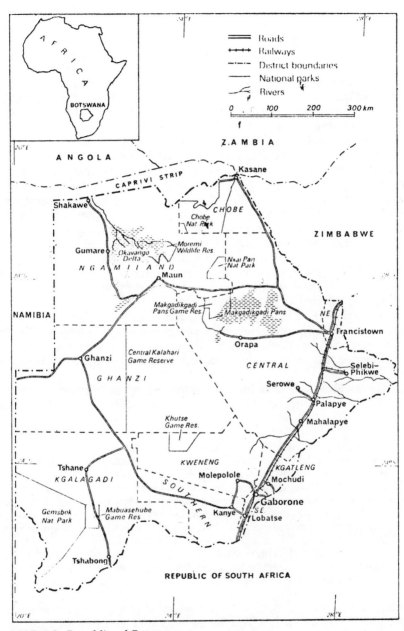

MAP 1.2. Republic of Botswana.
Source: Frontispiece, in Charles Harvey, ed., *Papers on the Economy of Botswana* (London: Heinemann, 1981), p. iii. Reprinted with permission.

in many rivers between October and May, but in the Kalahari there is never open water except in the numerous playas of pans after rainfall."[15]

Rainfall tends to be limited, uneven in its distribution, and variable. In the northern portions of the country, the annual average rainfall decreases from 25.6 inches (650 millimeters) at the northern border to 17.7 inches (450 millimeters) just north of the Makgadikgadi Pans. Rainfall in the east decreases from about 21.7 inches (551 millimeters) in the southeast to about 13.8 inches (350 millimeters) in the northeast. The western boundary of this zone is roughly 90 miles (145 kilometers) west of Gaborone and 150 miles (241 kilometers) west of Serowe.[16] The country is also subject to periodic drought conditions.

This pattern of rainfall and water availability is fundamental to the agricultural economy and population distribution. It accounts for a concentration of people and livestock in the eastern portion of the country because the amount of rainfall is greater there, more permanent water supplies are available from the rivers during the rainy season (October–March), and underground sources of water exist.

The natural vegetation pattern reflects these geographic and climatic features (see Map 1.3). The drier parts of the Kalahari Desert are shrub savanna, and the wetter parts are tree savanna. The moist portion of the northeast is tree savanna with mopane; only small areas of the country are forested or are grass savanna.

Infrastructure. The social infrastructure of transportation, communications, energy, education, and health reflects two things. One is the paucity or underdevelopment of those facilities at the time of independence; the other is the rapid development of the infrastructure since that time.

The level of infrastructural development when Botswana became independent may be indicated by a summary presented by President Khama several years later.

> The basic physical and social infrastructure was sadly deficient, if not almost totally lacking. Roads, and telecommunications, water and power supplies were totally inadequate to provide a base for industrial development. Most important of all the colonial Government failed to recognize the need to educate and train our people so they could run their own country. Not one single secondary school was completed by the colonial Government during the whole seventy years of British rule. Nor did we inherit any properly equipped institutions for vocational training even at the lowest level of artisan skills. The administration had at its disposal only the most rudimentary information on our national resources. The country was largely unmapped.[17]

Having such a base to start with has meant that a large proportion of development resources has had to be allocated to infrastructural development. One accounting put the proportion of public investment in infrastructure during 1976–1981 at 86 percent and estimated that 47 percent of 1979/1980–1984/1985 expenditures would be on roads, transport, and communications.[18]

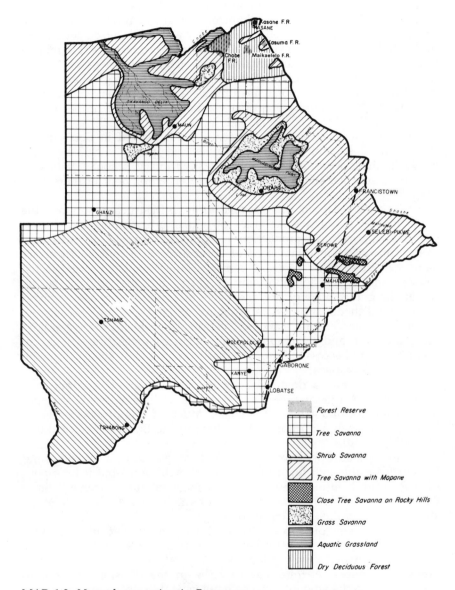

MAP 1.3. Natural vegetation in Botswana.
Source: Botswana, *National Development Plan 1976–81* (Gaborone: Government Printer, 1977), p. 3.

Although such expenditures detracted from investment in more directly productive activities, there was a need to create at least a basic physical underpinning of all economic activities. The results speak for themselves. In 1965, there were virtually no hard-surfaced all-weather roads, but by 1979, there were 686 miles (1,104 kilometers) of bitumen roads and 1,125 miles (1,810 kilometers) of gravel roads. Similarly, in 1966, electricity was generated by only a few widely dispersed generators; by 1980, the Botswana Power Corporation was producing 473.4 million kilowatt hours. Communications facilities—telephone, telegraph, radio/ telephone—also dramatically improved, and there was a great expansion in the number of educational institutions and pupils served. In 1966, there were 71,546 pupils in primary schools and 1,531 in secondary ones; by 1976, these numbers had increased to 125,588 and 9,558, respectively. In addition, a university was established in Botswana in 1971 with 42 students, and that number had grown to 465 by 1976. By 1982, there were 168,000 students in primary schools, 18,000 in secondary schools, and the university had an enrollment of more than 1,000.[19]

Agriculture, Mining, and Manufacturing. Infrastructure supports the more directly productive activities of agriculture, mining, and manufacturing. Agricultural production is composed largely of cattle and crops, and with a national herd of approximately 3 million, there are more than three cows for every person. Cattle have been raised in the country and region for hundreds of years, and the primary factors conditioning this activity are the need to productively use semiarid areas, establish an appropriate structure of land use and ownership, and maintain and expand markets. The primary problems revolve around the search for and development of water resources, the danger of overgrazing, and access to European markets along with the development of alternative markets.

Crop farming is dominated by the production of essential food crops, such as sorghum, millet, and maize, as well as of several varieties of domestic and indigenous vegetables. Much of this production is for local use although a portion is sold through the Botswana Agricultural Marketing Board.

Crop production involves upward of 80 percent of the rural households—although few of these are self-sufficient—but it is responsible for only a little over one-third of the total rural income.[20] Since the 1940s and 1950s, the agricultural sector's ability to feed the population, and create a surplus, has declined.[21]

The problems of crop production involve a number of issues. One is a degree of competition for land between crop and cattle producers, and another involves the availability of inputs, oxen, and fertilizer and extension services. A third has to do with the division of labor in agriculture and the amount of wage employment in Botswana and South Africa.[22]

The one area of natural resources in which Botswana is well endowed is that of minerals. Beginning in the late colonial period, exploration revealed considerable deposits of mineral resources and fossil fuel. There are copper and nickel deposits at Selebi-Phikwe as well as copper in the northwest, and large reserves of coal are known to exist in several places—although only one deposit, at Marupule near Mahalapye, has been developed. Most spectacular have been the discoveries of kimberlite pipes containing diamonds of both industrial and gem quality. The exploitation of such deposits at Orapa and Letlhakane in the north and Jwaneng in the southeast has provided continuing significant government revenues and money for public investment. The deposits also have attracted massive foreign private investment and bi- and multilateral aid.[23]

Manufacturing occupies a tertiary place in the economy and tends to be small, dependent, and "light." Most manufacturing focuses on reducing the amount of imported finished products even though most enterprises are foreign owned and import their raw materials. Total sales in 1975/1976 amounted to P 17.7 million, and the firms employed 2,564 people. The manufacturing sector is growing very slowly, a pattern that has been acceptable to the government.[24]

The type of manufacturing that has developed is the result of several factors. One is the smallness of the domestic market, but probably the most important factors are the country's proximity to the large manufacturing economy of South Africa and Botswana's membership in the customs union. These factors make manufacturing in Botswana uncompetitive, so the manufacturing enterprises tend to be located in areas where there are natural tariff barriers (e.g., transportation costs) or where Botswana crafts are in demand. In addition, a fair amount of the manufacturing is related to final-stage assembly or repacking bulk shipments for final consumption.[25]

The physical setting of geography and climate affects the infrastructure and the economy, and an examination of it begins to provide a baseline assessment of contemporary Botswana. Such an examination indicates the physical assets and established activities of the country, and it can also begin to generate the data upon which a more comprehensive description and analysis can be based. However, such a description also requires similar data from the social and political arenas.

Social and Political Settings

Human Resources. Human resources encompass population characteristics, including size, distribution, and growth. Botswana's population is small and unevenly distributed. At the time of the 1971 census, there were 620,000 inhabitants, including a resident Batswana population of 563,000, a resident alien population of 11,000, and 46,000 Batswana who were "temporarily absent"—mainly in South Africa.[26] By 1981, the population had increased to 936,000 persons, but the characteristics of large absentee and expatriate populations continued.[27]

About 85 percent of the people live in a corridor that runs north and south in the eastern portion of the country—where the water supply is permanent, the amount of rainfall is greater, arable land is available,

Serowe in the Central District, reputed to be the largest village in Africa.

and the infrastructure is more developed. This population is largely rural, although the pace of urbanization has quickened. By 1981, an estimated 16 percent of the total population lived in urban areas, a pattern that held true in this more populous area of the country as well. Urban growth averaged 10.7 percent per year between 1971 and 1981 compared with rural growth, which averaged 4.2 percent per year.

The population of Botswana is young—an estimated 50 percent of the population is twenty years of age or younger—and there are also significantly more females than males, particularly in the economically active age groups. This latter fact is accounted for by the large number of males who migrate for employment and indicates the fact that the women are greatly responsible for agricultural production and for caring for the young, old, and infirm. The overall picture is that "the de facto population age-sex pyramid has the truncated look of a nation just having been mauled by war."[28]

In rural areas, there is also an uneven distribution of the population. In 1971, 32.2 percent of the people lived in villages of 1,000 inhabitants or more, and 56.4 percent lived in settlements with a population of less than 500. In 1981, 2.8 percent lived in localities of 15,000 people or more, and 47 percent were counted in localities of 500 inhabitants or fewer.[29] The people in the smallest settlements included those living on the "lands" (arable areas), on cattle posts, and on freehold farms.[30] Although an increasing number of people were settling permanently on the lands, large numbers continued to divide their residential time between two or more locations (large villages, the lands, cattle posts).[31]

The geographical distinction among the people who live in urban areas and large and small villages coincides with other characteristics. Urban areas tend to have younger, better educated, and wealthier residents than the large villages do, and in turn, the people in the small villages tend to be older, less educated, and poorer than those in the large villages. In addition, there is an "extrarural" population of hunter-gatherers, and their access to the benefits of a settled life is even more limited than is the case for the small-village residents.[32]

Employment and Standard of Living. Ultimately, all of these resources result in patterns of employment and a standard of living—the quality of life. The most striking feature of life in Botswana is that the majority of the population must engage in a variety of occupations in order to provide family sustenance. For example, although over 80 percent of the rural population engages in agricultural production, this activity "contributed only 35 percent of total rural income, the most important supplement being 'transfers' into the household of some portion of the wages being paid to roughly 50,000 Batswana workers in South Africa and 49,000 in Botswana."[33] A large proportion of the people who work full-time in the cities have very direct connections to rural households: They may own cattle, they may remit wages to their families, their families may grow crops, or a combination of any of these possibilities may exist.

Thus, the quality of life has a very fluid and uncertain character. One observable feature is the mobility of the population and an oscillating pattern of internal and external migratory labor. Some of the workers move to obtain wage employment, and in agriculture, there is a seasonal shift to and from the lands areas, and some people follow the movement of the cattle as they search for grass and water.

Another notable feature of the quality of life is poverty. Although starvation is not a widespread problem or threat, except during long periods of drought, Botswana is a poor country. The revenues from mineral exploitation have increased the per capita income, but that increase has not resulted in a prosperous life for the majority of the population. The most comprehensive study of income shows that nearly half the rural population lives below a strict poverty datum line,[34] and one urban study indicates that two-thirds of the wage earners live below a more generous, but not opulent, poverty line.[35]

In addition, there is significant inequality in income distribution. The poorest 50 percent of the population shared 17.4 percent of total rural income; in contrast, the richest 10 percent had 42 percent of the total income.[36] But the standard of living of even the wealthier people is relatively modest. In 1975, only 500 rural households (out of 89,624) had incomes of P 8,690 or more, and in 1976, only about 3 percent of the urban wage/salary earners had an income of P 8,000 or more.[37]

Although economic growth and inflation have changed the absolute monetary figures, the pattern was little changed in 1983. Despite the government's continued emphasis on social justice, the standard of living continues to reflect a low income per household and a relative inequality in the distribution of income.[38]

Political Structures and Relations. The final element of the social and political settings—the political structures and their relationships—

provides the means through which society is knit together and through which resources and incomes are allocated. Botswana is a parliamentary democracy, and the representative institution on the national level is Parliament, which is made up of the National Assembly and the presidency, with elections being held at least every five years. The House of Chiefs represents the traditional tribal institutions on the national level and has advisory power on issues affecting traditional institutions.[39] The High Court, sitting in Lobatse, supervises the hierarchy of courts in the country. The national administrative system is overseen by an executive cabinet, and its day-to-day work is carried out by the Botswana Public Service, which operates under rules administered by the Directorate of Personnel in the Office of the President.

Local institutions are creations of the national government. The nine district and four town councils are responsible for a limited range of functions and operate through administrative staffs headed by council secretaries and other officers in the Unified Local Government Service. In addition, traditional structures, each headed by a chief, parallel the local councils in most areas outside of the towns. These structures are also creations of the national government and operate under statutory law. The supervision of local by national government is effected largely through the Ministry of Local Government and Lands. The primary officers and organizations involved are the district commissioners, district development committees, and land boards.[40]

Nongovernmental institutions and formal groups include the four political parties, various interest groups, and external entities. The two most important political parties are the Botswana Democratic party (BDP) and the Botswana National Front (BNF). The BDP has been the national and local governing party virtually since its inception, and it has dominated the National Assembly since independence. The BNF is the main opposition party, although it has mainly a regional base and is not an electoral threat on the national level. Interest groups include the Botswana Employers' Federation, trade unions, and groups of civil servants, teachers, and less-organized, but powerful, cattleowners. External entities include foreign investors. These companies are interested primarily in mining, but there are other investors as well, such as South African Breweries.

The most significant underlying political relationship is that between the organized BDP and its mass base. This relationship is the glue that binds the polity and is composed largely of cattleowners and a bureaucratic elite in the BDP persistently mobilizing the support of the noncattleowning subsistence farmers and the migratory laborers. This alliance provides the basis for the political dominance of the BDP. Its economic manifestation in rural areas is in the form of cattle being loaned by the elite to small farmers and in the form of employment on the cattle posts and in the shops owned by the large cattleowners. In addition, close working relationships on the national level among the BDP elite, senior civil servants, and mining concerns assure the financial base of government institutions. Subsidiary relationships on government boards and through consultation aid the formulation of government policy.

CLASS, POLITICS, AND DEVELOPMENT IN BOTSWANA: A POLITICAL ECONOMY APPROACH

The day-to-day content of the economic, social, and political situations defines the political economy of Botswana. In describing and analyzing the political economy, the theoretical perspective is largely implicit, but it must be recognized that the choices of descriptive categories and data are always rooted in an analytical perspective. The parameters of that analytical perspective must be explained, if briefly.

A political economy is composed of two sets of dynamic and interwoven relationships. One set is the relationship of the people to the natural world and other people while producing and distributing the material products of society. These relationships have to do with the ownership and control of the means of production and the perceptions leading to the actions of the people involved. The shared characteristics resulting from these relations, perceptions, and actions define different groups as classes. In capitalist societies such as Botswana, the primary class division is between some form of bourgeois and working-class groups.

The second set of relationships is political and is defined by the relationships between and among classes. Under capitalism, the primary factors are the domination of a bourgeois class and the articulation of that group with some form of working class. These relationships are institutionalized in the structures of government and the political parties, and they are structured by the day-to-day practices of classes regarding each other.

Classes and their politics therefore define a political economy, but three points need to be made about this definition. One is that this framework cannot be imposed by an observer; on the contrary, it is the constitution of classes and politics in history that suggests their definition and importance. Second, and related to the first point, the constitution of classes and politics in history suggests the expectation that the resulting relationships will be rich and multifaceted. Although the continuity of broad class constructs within major types of societies will be evident, the specific organization and activities of each will be diverse and complex. Third, this definition of a political economy implies a variety of historical possibilities. It does not presuppose or lead to any simple and crude determination of the past, present, or future. Instead, the definition of classes and politics opens up the possibility of alternatives in history by precisely defining what does determine the present, explains the past, and implies the future. The economic and political relationships in a political economy unfold and develop throughout their history, and moments of choice and change define their development.

The themes of class and state relationships recur in the chapters of this book. Chapter 2 provides a historical background and highlights the changes that made Bechuanaland a labor reserve colony in southern Africa. Chapter 3 summarizes the main elements of growth and change in the postcolonial period, and Chapters 4 and 5 describe and analyze the resulting maintenance of and change in class and state relations. Chapter 6 introduces the international dimension of Botswana's development, and all of these separate elements are knit together in Chapter 7.

2

Colonialism, Underdevelopment, and Nationalism in the Bechuanaland Protectorate

A survey of the preindependence period is necessary if one is to measure change in the contemporary era. In addition, such a survey makes it possible to identify the factors and processes that explain why change has, or has not, taken place. This chapter describes precolonial Tswana society, the impact of colonial rule on it, and the response of the people to that rule.

THE PRECOLONIAL PERIOD TO 1870

This description of African societies in the precolonial period does not differentiate among the principal Tswana societies or treat separately non-Tswana societies such as the Bayei, Basarwa, and Bakalanga. Although we are dealing with a number of distinct Tswana societies and states, they were related and sufficiently similar to be considered together, and although the non-Tswana societies remained distinct, the process of their incorporation into Tswana society means that their description may be merged with the discussion of that society.[1]

The territory of present-day Botswana has been inhabited for thousands of years.[2] Little is known about the origins or the social and political organization of the early peoples, but it is probable that the prehistoric populations came and went in response to ecological and sociopolitical conditions. The origin of the current population dates primarily from the eighteenth century. The main Tswana migration moved westward from South Africa, and it was stimulated by internal fission, competition from other African communities, and later, European pressure. By 1800, several related Tswana societies had been established and were expanding.[3]

Economic activity centered largely around the production and consumption of essential goods, food, clothing, and housing. This production involved cattle and goats, small-scale crop farming, hunting and gathering. The cycle of agricultural production depended upon uncertain and limited rainfall, which meant that cattle and people had to move frequently to find areas where grass and crops would grow, and the movement generally coincided with seasonal rainfall patterns. Residential concentrations became established near more-or-less-permanent water supplies and provided the focal point for political and social life.

The organization of each society and its economy was based on ethnicity and kinship, with a specific division of labor based on age and sex. In most areas, non-Tswana groups were subordinate to the Tswana, and the non-Tswana rendered tribute in the form of produce and/or labor.[4] Different male and female age groups performed various collective economic and defense functions. The older men hunted; young men and older boys looked after the cattle and small stock. Women and girls did the household tasks and had primary responsibility for child care and the crops.

The central political institution of each society was that of the kingship, a hereditary position with the royal line having divine sanction. The king was the embodiment of the community as a whole, and he was the guardian of the people, their livestock, and their land. The king's powers were all-encompassing in theory, but occasionally limited in practice, and included the power to allocate land for grazing, crops, and residence. The king played a central role in the agricultural cycle, announcing the planting season and receiving the "first fruits," and he was responsible for the defense of his people, mobilizing the males into an army when necessary. The king exercised his authority through a hierarchy of relatives and officials, including his close advisers and ward headmen. The latter had authority within a ward, a geographically specific place inhabited by a number of related households and the smallest political unit.

Paralleling the hierarchy of officials was a series of public forums. The *kgotla*, an assembly of adult males in which matters of public interest were discussed, met on the ward level through to the level of the whole state and introduced an open and democratic element into the system. Although the powers of the *kgotla* were advisory only, the king and his officials could use that forum to generate a consensus before taking action and to sense opposition to particular proposals. In addition, the *kgotla* was a venue for court cases.

The officials held authority partially because of the sanction of tradition embodied in the king and his subordinates, but they also tended to be substantial cattleowners. Cattle, unlike the land, were individually owned, and herds were divided up among a large number of clients who had the use of the cattle (as well as of some of the meat

Chief's *kgotla* (*left*) and house (*right*) in Molepolole.

and milk). In return for the use of cattle, noncattleowners were expected to provide political support for the officials who, in turn, were responsible for the welfare of the whole society.

Such relations between the king and the people extended to other areas as well. The Tswana collected tribute from the subordinate non-Tswana peoples, but within the Tswana community itself, tribute played an important role in the social and political relations. For example, the people might give portions of animals they killed in hunting (*sehuba*) or a portion of their crops to the king, till the fields of the king, or render service to the royal family.

Changes in each society resulted partly from a certain amount of tension within it. This tension found its origins in the distinction between the tribute-paying and the tribute-receiving classes and in the control exercised by the latter group. In addition, there was conflict within the ruling class over economic control and the distribution of authority. One result was a tendency toward fission in the society, i.e., the breaking away of a segment of the society to found a new one. A disgruntled minority, often led by a dissident member of the royal family, might move to a new area and establish an autonomous society, and most of the present-day Tswana tribes resulted from such a process. The Bangwato resulted from a split in the Bakwena society at the end of the eighteenth century, and the Batawana tribe was created later as a result of a further split in the Bangwato society. With large areas of land suitable for settlement, such fission was fairly common, and its possibility had the internal effect of forcing the kings to be responsive to some social pressure. Externally, it led to the expansion of Tswana economic and political institutions into areas that were occupied by less-organized and weaker societies. These societies then became subordinate units in the Tswana economy and state.

Similar societies existed in many parts of Africa during the pre-colonial period, and Samir Amin calls them "tributary social formations." They were marked by the existence of two major classes, "the peasantry, organized in communities, and the ruling class, which monopolizes the functions of the given society's political organization and exacts a tribute . . . from the rural communities."[5] It is important to note, however, that there was a considerable amount of intertwining of political and economic rights and relations between the two classes, which limited the extent to which exploitation could take place. For example, although the king had the power to allocate land, every tribesman had the right to sufficient land on which to graze cattle and grow crops.

The history of most of these Tswana societies was one of growth, expansion, and change, and their growth and development accelerated in the early to mid-nineteenth century as Tswana societies came into sustained contact with various European communities.[6] The technological innovations and manufactured products that became available were incorporated into the Tswana societies and increased their strength and prosperity. European rifles made hunting and defense much more efficient and productive, and the introduction of new agricultural tools (e.g., the plow) and techniques increased the possibility of greater food surpluses, which could be converted into European manufactured goods and food items. The development of an extensive wagon trade facilitated these developments and created many new opportunities, and the heyday of this growth probably extended into the 1890s, which marked the high point of the wagon trade from the Cape Colony to central Africa. The Bangwato reaped the main benefits of this particular trade.

Thus, most of the nineteenth century was a period of accelerated development and change. Although not without setbacks and some undesirable consequences, this change usually strengthened the Tswana societies and their ruling classes.

COLONIALISM AND UNDERDEVELOPMENT IN BECHUANALAND: 1870–1940

The ensuing period saw a reversal in the development of the Tswana societies. From the 1880s onward, Tswana autonomy eroded, and its dynamic base was undermined. As a result, Tswana societies were increasingly integrated into, or incorporated as subordinate entities of, the European imperial world.

Empire Building in Southern Africa: 1870–1895

The erosion of Tswana stability and independence was not a sudden phenomenon in the late nineteenth century, and indeed, the depiction of growth and prosperity must be tempered by two facts. One was the upheaval known as the *difaqane,* or forced migration, in South Africa. In the 1822–1836 period, this intra-African warfare disrupted some Tswana societies, and similar disturbances further north later in the century had comparable destabilizing effects. The second fact was that during the bulk of the century, the Tswana societies had been pressured by the expansion efforts of the Afrikaners in South Africa. The Afrikaners were descendants of Dutch settlers in the Cape region who moved into the interior in large numbers early in the nineteenth century to escape what they regarded as oppressive British rule. The Afrikaner economy was very similar to that of the Tswana, but the Afrikaners claimed large areas of land and African labor as their right. As early as the 1830s, their expansive tendencies brought them into contact and conflict with the Tswana, and this conflict persisted and was very costly for the Tswana societies. The ultimate cost was the fact that the societies were forced to enter into alliances with other Europeans who could resist the Afrikaner encroachment. It was after 1870, however, that intra-European rivalry for exclusive colonial possessions intensified, and what was becoming known as Bechuanaland became part of this territorial struggle.

It was not that the area inhabited by the Tswana was in and of itself desirable real estate. Although some portions of it were suitable for ranching, and in the late 1860s and early 1870s it was thought the area might contain significant gold deposits,[7] the importance of the territory centered on its geopolitical position and terrain. Access to the interior of Africa depended on ox-drawn wagons, which required a relatively flat, unobstructed terrain, and this type of topography existed in Bechuanaland. The area thus attracted the attention of those Europeans who were interested in occupying central Africa.

Because of the enormous wealth being generated after the discovery of diamonds at Kimberley in 1870, the British interests in South Africa began to envision other mining ventures and European settlement in the interior of Africa, and the mineral revolution in southern Africa, upon which much else depended, accelerated with the proclamation of the Witwatersrand of South Africa as a gold-mining area in 1886. The vision was colonization northward into what later became Northern and Southern Rhodesia. This colonization would be undertaken, under the protection of the British Crown, by a monopoly chartered company, led by Cecil Rhodes, which would provide the necessary administrative and political organization and organize a full range of profitable investments.

The equally expansive Afrikaner republics in the Transvaal, and the Afrikaners to the west and south who encroached on the "road to the north," represented a threat to such development. In addition, there was concern that the Germans, who annexed South West Africa in 1884, might, in conjunction with the Afrikaner republics, extend into the interior and thus block the northern route.

Missionaries had been long established among the Tswana, and they mounted their own campaign to persuade the British government to intervene against the Afrikaners—and to some extent against the machinations of the colonial interests in the Cape Colony. The missionaries were important advocates in Britain and in persuading two of the Tswana kings to ask for British protection.

The outcome was the declaration of a British crown colony in southern Bechuanaland in 1885 (British Bechuanaland, which became part of the Cape Colony in 1895 and is now part of the Cape Province of South Africa) and a protectorate in northern Bechuanaland (now Botswana). The protectorate secured British influence in the region and access to central Africa; it also paved the way for the extension of Cape colonial commercial ventures. From the point of view of the Tswana, it eased the pressure of Afrikaner encroachment from the southeast and the possibility of German pressure from the west.

The constitutional position and future of Bechuanaland, however, were somewhat indeterminate in 1885. The chief's interpretation of the protectorate was that it affected only external affairs and left them free to handle their internal affairs independently. The British government in London, particularly the treasury, wanted to ensure the integrity of the territory for British interests but was reluctant to commit resources for its development or the manpower for its administration. British officers in the field, however, felt it was necessary to develop an administrative system that would establish their authority and clearly separate the political and administrative system from commercial operations.

Another factor was the British South Africa Company (BSAC), which was chartered in 1889 and headed by Rhodes. The company's vision was to unify commercial and political operations under its authority. It sought to persuade the British government to give the company unfettered authority to negotiate concessions with the Africans and offered to undertake the administration of the territories. Although this offer was attractive to the treasury, because it would have eliminated the costs of providing an administrative structure, it provoked the hostility of Tswana leaders, the missionaries, and some British colonial officials.

British government orders in council in 1890 and 1891, and proclamations implementing them, seemed to establish the principle of a British government administration, but they did not clarify the relationship between British officials and African chiefs. In addition, they did not settle the question of the role of the BSAC. In 1894, the company formally requested an assurance from the British government that the administration of Bechuanaland would be given to the company at some point, and this request finally forced a decision.

Intense lobbying on all sides in 1894 and 1895, including a visit to England by three of the chiefs, resulted in a decision that the British government would maintain the administrative system and the chiefs would be allowed to rule as they had within the existing tribal territories. The BSAC was granted authority in areas where concessions had been negotiated, but this authority was revoked after a disastrous raid into South Africa, which was led by the company's agent in Bechuanaland, Dr. Leander Jameson, in December 1895. Henceforth, the protectorate would be the responsibility of the British government. The only lasting, and not unimportant, concessions to the company were three blocks of prime ranchland (Tuli, Gaberones, and Lobatse blocks) and a strip of land on which the railway from South Africa to Rhodesia had been built.[8]

At the same time that these political relationships were taking shape, important changes occurred in the economy, three being particularly noteworthy. First, the building of the railway undermined the commercial activity that had built up in the previous period around the wagon trade. The need for fresh oxen, food, and wagon repair services disappeared, and whatever prosperity and development these activities had generated were eliminated. Second, in 1896 a rinderpest epidemic decimated Tswana cattle herds and decreased the Tswanas' ability to derive a livelihood through agricultural production or by selling cattle. Third, the concessions of land to the BSAC and the confirmation of the Tati Concession (which alienated land in the northeast) created land pressure in some areas, and the drawing of boundaries around tribal territories in 1899 limited the available land elsewhere. Taxation imposed in the same year also increased the economic pressures on Tswana societies. The economic response was an attempt to find substitute activities, but the Tswana were less than successful in this attempt, for their ability to engage in discretionary economic activity was being rapidly undermined.

Colonialism and Underdevelopment: 1895–1940

The establishment of British government control meant that Bechuanaland became a part of the British Empire. The question remained as to what specific niche the protectorate would occupy. British interests in the region were primarily in central Africa and South Africa. Bechuanaland, then, once the road to the north was secure, was not viewed as being of primary importance. What was required was that one, it should be stable and secure, two, it should be self-supporting and not become a permanent ward of the British treasury, and three, its organization and economy should complement British interests in the region.

The first requirement was met by the establishment of a modest administrative apparatus, including a relatively large law and order component, and an appropriate political organization. The second resulted in the imposition of taxation to pay for the administrative system, and the third meant that the economy and society became intertwined with the development of the economy of South Africa.

The political organization of the protectorate as a British territory had internal and external dimensions. Internally, "parallel rule" existed until the 1930s. A resident commissioner, based in the "imperial reserve" in Mafeking, South Africa, had authority over a modest staff of European officers, the most important of which were the district commissioners. These commissioners were magistrates in addition to being administrators. A parallel African organization was also created. Each of the Tswana tribal organizations was recognized and retained authority under the supervision of the new European layer of administration. The Europeans supervised the African administrators in all cases involving Europeans and in ensuring uniform taxation and expenditure patterns in the protectorate as well as coordinating the role of the territory in the empire.

Overall coordination and supervision for the protectorate was institutionalized in 1920 with the creation of separate native and European advisory councils.[9] Both councils had "official" (government officer) majorities and were advisory only. Lacking legislative power, the councils often became a place for the resident commissioner to announce his plans and to persuade the chiefs to accept their rather subordinate role. Some chiefs saw their participation as an infringement on their authority and participated sporadically, if at all. The Bangwato, for example, did not participate regularly until 1940.

The political subordination of the African layer of government was substantial despite appearances. In the 1930s, this subordination was finally determined in a Privy Council case, the conclusion of which was essentially that "His Majesty has unfettered and unlimited power to legislate for the government of and administration of justice among the Native tribes in the Bechuanaland Protectorate."[10]

Externally, the protectorate was an appendage of South Africa in the British Empire. The Act of Union in 1910, which created modern South Africa, actually provided for the incorporation of the High Commission Territories, of which Bechuanaland was one, into South Africa. Although this provision was never carried out, it is indicative of the attitude toward the independent existence of Bechuanaland.

In addition, several policies and arrangements firmly created a political and economic intertwining of Bechuanaland and South Africa.[11] The recruitment of European officials was undertaken in South Africa for the most part, with the exception of the very top ones (e.g., the resident commissioner). The British representative to South Africa was, until 1963, also the chief administrative officer of the protectorate. As such, he reported to the Dominions, not the Colonial, Office, and the territory was therefore treated in England as part of South Africa, not as a separate colonial entity. The administrative headquarters of the protectorate was in Mafeking, South Africa. Furthermore, the main customs union agreement of 1910, while relieving the British administration of the costs of collecting customs revenue and providing a major share of the government's yearly recurrent revenues, had the effect of generating and maintaining the protectorate's dependence on South Africa.

The primary activity of the Bechuanaland administration was to collect taxes to maintain a modest number of officers and law and order. During the whole colonial period, approximately 75 percent of all expenditures went to "administrative" costs; relatively small amounts went to developing the social infrastructure or the country's productive capacity in agriculture or manufacturing. Even the modest levels of public expenditure had to be supported by tax revenues. Thus, in 1899, a hut tax of £1.00 was imposed, and such taxation became permanent and increased in 1919 with the addition of a "native" tax, which was initially a surcharge of three shillings on each £1 of hut tax.[12]

The new taxation was an addition to the continuation of the payment of traditional tribute. Furthermore, the new taxes must be seen in the context of changes in patterns of consumption. One such change was a new demand for education, which required special tribal levies, and another, which began in the nineteenth century, was that a range of imported goods (e.g., processed food, clothes, and guns) had become part of a modest standard of living for many people.

Satisfying these patterns of consumption had been possible until 1900 through discretionary (i.e., voluntary) participation in the wider market economy. Short-term migration to the diamond and gold fields of South Africa or the selling of some crops or cattle and goats had provided the necessary cash. Now, however, the new taxation transformed discretionary into nondiscretionary (i.e., involuntary) participation. This change created the basis of the migratory labor system[13] and began the separation of economic rights from political rights and obligations.

Essentially, the taxation "forced upon the people the necessity of finding a regular sum of money each year."[14] In a purely voluntary environment, with all other factors being equal, there were a number of activities that would generate the required cash, such as the sale of crops, cattle, and manufactured goods; engaging in trade; and employment in Bechuanaland. All other factors were not equal, however, and the environment increasingly became an involuntary one.

In agriculture, natural and political factors eliminated or drastically reduced the people's ability to market their commodities. Only a limited range of crops could be produced, little investment was made in improving crop production, and the 1896–1897 rinderpest epidemic decimated the cattle herds. Although there were new opportunities to market cattle in South Africa early in the twentieth century, the increasingly protected development of South Africa's agriculture and the rapid development of that country's infrastructure meant that Bechuanaland's position in regard to the sale of its produce was decreasingly competitive.

One significant factor in the reduction of the protectorate's ability to earn income from agriculture was purely political. In 1924, South Africa imposed weight restrictions, which were increased in 1926, on the importation of cattle from Bechuanaland. These restrictions drastically reduced the ability of the African, but not resident Afrikaner, farmers to market their cattle despite their attempts to find an alternative market. The 1923 levels of recorded exports were not again reached until the restrictions were lifted in 1942.[15]

Engaging in trade could be a means for some people to earn a living, but the opportunity to do so was restricted. Even chiefs were denied trading licenses, and a series of discriminatory acts (such as the 1923 Credit Sales to Natives Proclamation) had the effect of preventing Africans from engaging in the money economy as traders.[16] Even as late as 1949, there were only a total of ten African-owned stores in Bechuanaland as opposed to 155 European-owned ones.[17]

Cattle in the Central District.

A result of all these factors was that there was a very limited number of opportunities to work for wages in Bechuanaland itself. In an economy with fewer than 200 stores, only a few freehold farms, a miniscule government structure and budget, and no manufacturing, a large working class could not develop. The estimates of the number of employed people in 1947 totaled 4,860; 41 percent of these were employed in agriculture, and 30 percent were in domestic service.[18] Employment in the country did not increase until the 1960s, and even in 1964, only 31,600 people were employed, including the self-employed and the white-collar employees in government service.[19]

There was one avenue of relief: There was a strong demand, particularly in mining, for foreign workers in South Africa.[20] This demand was for relatively unskilled labor at the lowest possible wage, and it formed the basis for a large amount of migratory and short-term employment. Such employment meant that wages could be paid as though the worker were single and avoided the need for the infrastructure and fringe benefits that permanent employment would require. These factors were uppermost in the minds of employers. In 1944, for example, they were articulated as follows:

> It is clearly to the advantage of the mines that Native Labourers should be encouraged to return to their homes after the completion of the ordinary period of service. The maintenance of the system under which the mines are able to obtain unskilled labour at a rate less than that ordinarily paid in industry depends upon this, for otherwise the subsidiary means of

subsistence would disappear and the labourer would tend to become a permanent resident upon the Witwatersrand, with increased requirements.[21]

The demand for labor in South Africa and the need to earn cash in Bechuanaland quickly created a pattern of oscillating migratory labor that touched almost all the people who lived in the protectorate. In 1930, 4,012 Batswana were employed in South Africa, and the number increased to 10,314 in 1935 and to 18,411 in 1940. In 1943, nearly half of all males aged fifteen to forty-four were away from the protectorate.[22] The protectorate government, although bemoaning the necessity of this type of employment, aided in organizing and facilitating the recruitment of labor and attempted to protect the interests of the migrants and their families.

The social and political processes of colonization therefore transformed the previously independent and dynamic societies into dependent entities, and their dependence was brought about because their ability to support themselves was progressively undermined. Although the main types of agricultural production continued more or less as before, the additional requirements related to taxation and a changed standard of living could not be met by this means. Other opportunities to meet these requirements in Bechuanaland—selling cattle, engaging in trade, or working for wages—were either progressively eliminated or were too limited to meet the increased demand for cash.

The result was migration for employment in the mines of South Africa. From the migrant's point of view, the wage received was a necessary and an additional amount to the total household income. Although some portion of the wage could be used to purchase and take home consumer goods that were more than simple necessities, the bulk of the wage had to go for household subsistence. The combination of agricultural production in Bechuanaland and the migratory wages made up the amount that was necessary to sustain households.

For the mining industry in South Africa, the migratory labor was an important basis for profitability. Wages did not have to be subsistence level because the costs of having and rearing children, feeding and housing families, and caring for the elderly and disabled were largely borne by the people in the protectorate. In addition, it was unnecessary for the South African government to provide educational, health, and other infrastructural services for those households, which meant the mining industry did not have to pay higher taxes to support those services. In several ways, therefore, the mines could make higher profits than would have been possible if they had had to pay the full necessary costs of ensuring a continual supply of labor. The result was development for South Africa and underdevelopment for Bechuanaland. The protectorate had become a labor reserve colony.[23]

The economic, social, and political consequences of this underdevelopment in the protectorate were enormous. Economically, stagnation and underdevelopment in relation to the region and the world resulted. The exodus of active male laborers undermined the agricultural and manufacturing sectors and meant that Bechuanaland was subsidizing the cost of labor in South Africa. The able worked elsewhere, and the costs of child care and care for the old and infirm had to be met by the now crippled economy of the territory.

In addition, the low level of internal production did not justify expenditures on the social infrastructure. The maintenance of migratory labor required only minimal educational and transportation systems, but it also meant that the government's coffers received only enough money to pay basic administrative costs. Although several of the tribes did attempt to develop, particularly in the area of education,[24] their resources and capacities were severely limited.

The social consequences were equally striking as normal family life and household activities were disrupted. With the men away for eleven months a year, the women had to do the work associated with crop production, cope with generating subsistence, manage the household, and attempt to maintain some kind of social continuity. In addition, the migrant labor system increased the amount of debilitating diseases, such as tuberculosis and syphilis, as well as prostitution and crime.[25]

The political aspect of underdevelopment paralleled the economic and social aspects as existing political relations were not replaced but adapted to the new situation. The authority of the colonial government ensured control of the chiefs and, through them, the masses, but the political relationship between the chiefs and the people was not structurally transformed. The chiefs now facilitated migration and collected taxes in addition to collecting their traditional tribute through the exercise of precolonial political relations.

Tswana society was thus changed at its economic and social base. Formerly self-sufficient peasants in a tributary society were now partly proletarianized, and they became a "peasantariat,"[26] adapting peasant production and wage work into a new form of working-class existence. Because of this adaptation of previous political and economic relations, their new life as wage earners was not dominant in their political outlook. Likewise, although chiefs and other traditional authorities lost their independence, this loss happened in such a way as to mask this very real shift.

NATIONALISM IN BECHUANALAND: 1895–1966

The new social and political confusion was the basis for the apparent docility of the people in the protectorate during the colonial period— and beyond—which can be better illustrated by looking at nationalism in Bechuanaland during the colonial period. For this purpose, nationalism may be defined as the struggle of sociopolitical groups to protect or extend their identity, autonomy, and independence. Such nationalism has a social basis in the structure of society, may have various overlapping geographical boundaries, and may be localized or exist on the level of the nation state. During the colonial period in Bechuanaland, various forms of nationalism emerged in response to the social and political structure of colonial society.

Threads of Nationalist Development: 1895–1940

Clearly, the big losers in the colonial period were the self-sufficient peasants who were coerced into oscillating migration and low-wage employment. These people, the peasantariat, were the primary victims of underdevelopment, but they were also the least organized in expressing their interests and dissent.

Such expression was not absent, however. At times, the peasantariat "voted with its feet" through more or less permanent, often illegal, emigration, which was one of the concerns that stimulated I. Schapera's study of migrant labor in the 1940s. On the other hand, it was periodically necessary for the colonial authorities to persuade, cajole, and threaten people in order to get them to sign on for a contract period when insufficient numbers of workers volunteered, and in South Africa, despite legal barriers and the rigid structure of the compound system, resistance occurred. Work stoppages, protests, and other forms of struggle against work conditions and low wages became a part of going to the mines.[27]

The peasantariat did not, however, develop any kind of consistent organization, nor did one develop outside the class to represent its interests in agricultural and wage employment. The peasantariat was almost completely illiterate and widely dispersed in rural areas. The oscillating character of migrant labor and the laborers' dispersal to a large number of mines were also disorganizing, so activities in agriculture and wage employment were not of the type that would generate organization. The people who could form an organization and express demands, because of their position in society, did not do so explicitly to represent the peasantariat. These were the chiefs and other members of the traditional hierarchy—and later, the modernizing colonial elites who were employed in low-level, white-collar jobs.

Throughout the first part of the colonial period, the chiefs acted individually and collectively to prevent their own absolute subordination to Britain and the dissolution of their respective tribal nations. The successful trip of three chiefs to Britain in 1895 to request direct British government rather than BSAC administration must be seen in this context. The chiefs and the administration were periodically at odds over issues of tribal budgetary affairs, judicial practices, and political affairs until the 1930s, when the British government was moved to act once and for all to establish its authority over the chiefs in the tribal territories. Using the opportunity of the Pim Report's recommendations, the administration introduced ordinances in 1934 and 1938 to bureaucratize the chiefs and take away their formal political and financial independence. Two chiefs, of the Bangwato and Bankwaketse tribes, unsuccessfully protested the 1934 ordinances.[28]

The most protracted struggle engaging the chiefs and the peasantariat was that over incorporation into South Africa. The South African demand that the British High Commission Territories be absorbed by

South Africa received a sympathetic ear in some quarters in Britain, and the consistent struggle of the chiefs against incorporation occupied much of the nationalist thrust after 1910.[29]

What all the manifestations of nationalism had in common was the protection of the separate existence of the protectorate and, within the protectorate, of the separate existence and autonomy of the constituent units, the tribes—their territories and social and political institutions. This nationalism was based upon the political support of the peasantariat, but it mainly addressed issues concerning the status and independence of the tribal institutions and thus was centered on the chiefs and their hierarchies. This form of nationalism was somewhat limited in its demands and vision. It did not incorporate demands for the independence of the nation of Bechuanaland or for significant economic and political changes in the territory. Its demands were made in the context of a colonial society.

Such was not the case for the third group that emerged during the colonial era, which increasingly criticized colonialism and colonial nationalism, and eventually argued for national independence and significant internal change. This group was a product of colonial society yet stood in opposition to its continuation.

The introduction of a market economy and European administration to Bechuanaland required a small number of people to work in institutions related to them. In 1943, Schapera noted this development.

> The Government employs Native clerks, interpreters, orderlies, and agricultural demonstrators; the missions have introduced the vocations of clergyman and evangelist; the hospitals and medical officers train and employ nurses and dispensers; education has created a small class of teachers, both male and female; the local European residents employ storeassistants, domestic servants, and cattle-herds; the Chiefs have their secretaries and tax-collectors; and some people work for themselves as dressmakers, masons, carpenters, thatchers, or transport riders.[30]

In addition, a number of protectorate citizens found similar employment in South Africa.

These people shared the poverty of the peasantariat but were in a different position. They held jobs that placed them in close contact with Europeans, and they could see that their opportunities for education and advancement were limited by social and political, not natural, factors. Faced with racial discrimination and social barriers in attempting to develop their skills, they made demands that went to the heart of colonial society. In addition, their type of work began to stimulate the development of organizational skills that would be useful in organizing political activity. Finally, their future depended largely on developing skills and experience in the new institutions, not in the traditional or tribal institutions. This fact created the real possibility that they would find themselves in conflict with the chiefs and the tribal hierarchy.[31]

In the years up to World War II, these people were not very active politically. Although growing in number and influence, they were not well organized and were geographically dispersed. Perhaps most important, the period was still dominated by the transition from a peasant society to a peasantariat one and the clear political domination of the chiefs. Schapera noted that "almost every Native remains primarily a herdsman and cultivator; and the specialist calling in which he may also be engaged is still supplementary to his farming activities and has by no means taken their place. A backward headman of a large group possesses far more authority in tribal affairs than a teacher or artisan, unless the latter is himself a man of high rank."[32] This situation was to change, partly in response to changes in the postwar world and partly because increasingly, the teachers and artisans, the new social strata, came to be led by men who had traditional status.

Nationalism and Independence: 1940–1966

The post–World War II period was different. The world was not the same, and "winds of change" began sweeping the colonial world. Independence for India in 1947 gave stimulus to hopes elsewhere in the British Empire, and Britain began implementing "colonial development" schemes and programs of political decolonization. The speed and nature of decolonization depended upon the particular circumstances of each colonial territory. In Bechuanaland, the nature and pace of anticolonial political development depended primarily on the internal situation, which has been already outlined, and developments in South Africa.

Two main events in 1948 sparked the era of nationalist politics in Bechuanaland, which ended with the independence of Botswana in 1966. One was what would appear to be the unremarkable event that while studying in England, Seretse Khama married Ruth Williams, an Englishwoman. The second was the victory of the National party in the South African general election.

Seretse Khama's marriage was unremarkable except for the fact that he was heir to the chieftaincy of the Bangwato tribe, and it was not clear what the response of the tribe would be. There was hostility from his uncle and regent, Tshekedi Khama, and there was a division among the tribesmen over the marriage. At the same time, the National party in South Africa began creating the system of apartheid in that country, which was to relegate Africans to not only de facto but also legal and permanent subordinate status. The Bantustans, all-black enclaves that supply cheap black labor, and the legal framework of racial separation, including a ban on mixed marriages, were the system's mechanisms. Bechuanaland, along with the other two High Commission Territories of Basutoland (now Lesotho) and Swaziland, were clearly viewed as elements in South Africa's apartheid strategy.

The marriage of an African chief to a white woman was vehemently denounced in South Africa. One result was a renewed South African call that the High Commission Territories be transferred to South Africa as provided for in the 1910 Act of Union. The British government vacillated on the future of the territory and sought to defuse the issue of Seretse Khama's marriage. It did so in 1950 by banning Khama from Bechuanaland for a period of five years and by not responding directly to the issue of incorporation. The Conservative government went further in 1951 and 1952, telling Khama he would never be allowed to return and issuing a British government order in council barring his assumption of the chieftaincy or holding any formal position in the tribe. Serious disturbances occurred in the Bangwato territory as a result of this order, as by this time, the tribe had swung its support to Khama.

The British government undoubtedly was greatly concerned about its relations with South Africa. Why else would it treat a potentially very moderate African nationalist leader so shabbily when, at the same time, it accepted much more radical African leaders elsewhere on the continent? But Britain could not remain indecisive on the issue of incorporation, and gradually its actions moved in the direction of more self-government and eventual independence rather than incorporation.

There were two main reasons why independence became the wave of the future in Bechuanaland. One was the fact that there was a deep and persistent hostility in Bechuanaland toward incorporation, and chiefs and other people persistently argued against it. Second, other African nationalist leaders in the region and on the continent viewed the creation of apartheid with alarm and put pressure on Britain—in Britain and in international forums such as the United Nations—to prevent its extension to the High Commission Territories. Given this level of pressure on Britain, it would appear that South Africa must have come to the conclusion that pursuing incorporation was not worth the significant strain on that country's relations with Britain that doing so would cause and that other means, economic pressure, for example, could secure South Africa's interests in the region.

British policy therefore moved gradually, but almost inevitably, toward a process of decolonization. In 1951, a Joint Advisory Council, which brought together the formerly separate African and European advisory councils, was created. In 1956, Seretse Khama was allowed to return to Bechuanaland with his family on condition that neither he nor his children would claim the chieftaincy. He assumed the vice-chairmanship of the Bangwato Tribal Council, and from that time on, he took a leading role in domestic politics. In December of 1960, it was announced that a legislative council would be created, and in 1961, responsibility for the protectorate was shifted to the Colonial Office, which marked the end of Britain's interest in incorporation.[33]

Once the process of constitutional and political change began, its pace was very rapid. The Bechuanaland Peoples' party was created at the same time as the creation of a legislative council was announced, and Seretse Khama and others formed the Bechuanaland Democratic party in January 1962. Legislative and executive councils were created in June 1961, and constitutional discussions in 1963 resulted in a British commitment to grant internal self-government by a legislative assembly elected on the basis of universal adult suffrage. Assembly elections were held on 1 March 1965, and self-government was attained on 23 March. Independence talks were held in London in February 1966, and independence was granted on 30 September. Local government elections were held in 1966 as district and town councils came into existence. The pace of change was breathtaking given the history of the protectorate.

The political organization of this change was through political parties.[34] The Bechuanaland Peoples' party, later the Botswana Peoples' party (BPP), was formed in 1960, and its leaders were from the white-collar group created during the colonial era. P. G. Matante and Motsamai Mpho both had working experience in South Africa, and the third leader, K. T. Motsete, had a master's degree and was one of the early members of a small group with that level of education.

The BPP was anticolonial and demanded independence and a much reduced role for the traditional authorities. It sought to mobilize the workers and the emerging middle class in support of these demands[35] and enjoyed initial success, particularly in mobilizing members in urban and semiurban areas along the railway. Indeed, it organized large and impressive anticolonial demonstrations in Francistown and Lobatse in 1963, and Matante represented the BPP twice before the United Nations Committee on Colonialism. At its height, the party is reported to have had seventeen branches in Bechuanaland and five in Johannesburg.[36]

However, the BPP had difficulty in organizing the peasantariat. It focused on semiurban areas, and various obstacles were put in its path in tribal areas.[37] In addition, it was struck by a series of internal disputes. Mpho left the BPP in 1962 to form the Botswana Independence party (BIP), Matante and Motsete expelled each other in 1964, and the effectiveness of the BPP began to decline.

Nonetheless, the BPP did stimulate the formation of a more moderate party in 1962, the Bechuanaland Democratic party (BDP), which led the country to independence. The core of the BDP consisted of members of the Legislative Council, "all younger men of professional or traditional status in their respective Tribes. Several were school teachers."[38] By 1965, there were twenty-six BDP members of the Legislative Assembly, all of whom had some secondary education:

> Two were hereditary tribal leaders; twelve had experience as teachers under the colonial regime; nine had some form of employment with tribal administration; and four were employed by the colonial administration in some capacity. Five had experience as members of their respective tribal councils, while six served on either the African Advisory Council or the Legislative Council or both. Two had military experience during the Second World War.[39]

The leading figure in the BDP was Seretse Khama, who personified the party's emerging position of combining traditional legitimacy and peasantariat support with modern education and life. Others in the leadership cadre were either people of traditional economic (cattle-

1974 BDP poster picturing then-President Seretse Khama.

owning) and political standing or who occupied roles based on their education. Many of the leaders combined these attributes.

Little was needed to persuade the peasantariat that its future lay in loyalty to such a leadership cadre. Many of the leaders had agricultural contact with the peasantariat, and for most of the peasantariat, loyalty to the BDP was a simple extension of existing loyalties. On the other hand, to follow the BPP would have entailed breaking existing political relations, and in that sense, the constituted order of things would have been challenged. Such a dramatic break would have been uncharacteristic of the peasantariat; its natural affinity was with the BDP.

The organization of the BDP reflected both the nature of its leadership and this social base. Local notables in electoral constituencies organized their support for the BDP, and public meetings served the party as the *kgotla* served the chiefs. On the national level, the party was rather loosely organized as a coalition of notables under the leadership of the politically skillful Seretse Khama, and his vice-chairman, Q.K.J. Masire, played a strong organizing role. With a moderate program and this organization, leadership, and social base, the BDP quickly became the dominant party and was largely unchallenged by opposition parties except in the northeastern part of the country. The BDP swept the 1965 elections, winning twenty-eight out of thirty-one seats and 80.4 percent of the votes cast by 75 percent of the eligible electorate.[40]

The BDP was committed to achieving independence and to economic growth through mineral exploration combined with the commercialization of agriculture, particularly cattle production. The means to accomplish these aims would be a strong central government and elected local governments with tribal groups taking a "secondary place." Such objectives would be pursued in the "gradual but sure" way of building on existing structures.[41] The BDP moved quickly to act on its goals even before independence by creating local councils and by passing the Chieftainship Act of 1965, which essentially retained tribal government but made it subordinate to the central government.

As these developments occurred, a new party was formed in 1965. The Botswana National Front (BNF) was founded by Kenneth Koma, a socialist, and was based on the view that the BDP did not represent the real interests of the peasantry.[42] The BNF fielded seven candidates in the 1966 local government elections but won no seats. Its fortunes did not rise until Chief Bathoen Gaseitsiwe joined the party following his disaffection with the BDP—that event, however, occurred after independence.

UNDERDEVELOPMENT IN COLONIAL BECHUANALAND: A SUMMARY

The history of colonial Bechuanaland provides a background to development in the contemporary period, and the environment (economic, social, and political) with which the government of the newly independent country of Botswana was faced was the product of this history. But the same history also reveals the underlying dynamics that govern the changes in society. The new government of Botswana itself, in other words, was part of this history, and postindependence changes in it and the nation were based on the preceding period.

The environment created during the colonial period was one of underdevelopment. All development in the powerful British Empire centered on Britain itself, which led to the underdevelopment of its constituent units. For Bechuanaland, the underdevelopment was dramatic as the protectorate's economy and society were largely focused on developing the mining and manufacturing economy of South Africa.

Although the mechanism was economic, the process included coercive taxation and restrictions on economic activity, and this economic coercion was organized through the colonial political state. The consequences of this colonial policy were enormous. Having had a developing economy, society, and polity in the late nineteenth century, Bechuanaland now was wholly dependent on South Africa and Britain. The nondevelopment of Bechuanaland's economy meant that it was a poor country by the mid-twentieth century.

Thus, the labor reserve economy was the consequence of a social and political process as its primary characteristics of low-wage, male migratory labor and the enormous burdens placed on women did not come about spontaneously. But the consequences of this process did not result in a situation that was purely static. The realities of the labor reserve economy were the creation of new social strata and new economic and political relationships. The transformation of a self-sufficient peasantry into a semiproletarianized working class (the peasantariat) created a new social group with its own interests and dynamics. New types of professional and educational elites also emerged in the context of a transformed and redefined tribal hierarchy. The emergence of these groups and their activities in the colonial context describes the colonial polity and the course of nationalism. The independence era, therefore, began with this existing and dynamic economic, social, and political base, which has underlain the course of change in contemporary Botswana.

3

Political Evolution in Contemporary Botswana

It is clear that the state has played a central role in postcolonial Botswana. The weakness of the internal economy's infrastructure, markets, and productive capacity and its external dependence created a need for collective action. The absence of social infrastructure left Botswana without enough qualified personnel to successfully develop a private economy, and the organizational weakness of the political elite in political parties and the special place of the bureaucracy in that elite encouraged the creation and maintenance of relatively elaborate and powerful state institutions. Given these circumstances, a postcolonial structure in which the state played a secondary role would have been very surprising.

SOCIOCULTURAL CONTEXT

The sociocultural context of contemporary Botswana includes dimensions of individual and group identity, organization, and action. Its origins are found in the history of colonialism, in the way in which "rigid systems of colonial control affect the conscious self-identities" and behavior of "peoples whose existence is for the most part lived out in the lowlands of colonial domination." This culture, "in the heart of darkness," to use Hoyt Alverson's vivid imagery, encompasses ethnicity (ethnic identity and its significance), religion, art, sport, and associations of sociocultural diversity.[1]

Ethnicity

The population of Botswana is overwhelmingly African, but within that African population there are a number of ethnic communities. The most prominent are the eight major Tswana tribes, which share a common historical origin, language, social organization, and culture. To say that there are eight Tswana tribes is not to say that they are absolutely separate or inherently competitive. These groups are interrelated and represent a more or less single family of people, and distinctions among

35

Citizens of Botswana.

A Botswana man.

them take on the character of intrafamilial, rather than absolute, differences. There is cooperation as well as conflict among the tribes.

Non-Tswana African ethnic groups have at least some potentially conflicting relationship with the Tswana as historically, the Tswana conquered and incorporated non-Tswana groups as subordinate entities. The persistence of Basarwa/Khoisan, Bayei, and Bakalagali identities is a reminder of such Tswana conquests. The Kalanga people in the northeastern part of the country are another distinct group, and some of them feel they have specific problems and are distinctly subordinate to and competitive with the Tswana.

There are also South African and Zimbabwean populations, some of whom have become citizens of Botswana. Some native Batswana view these "paper citizens," who often occupy reasonably high positions, as opportunists who have adopted Botswana citizenship simply for convenience. Other people worry about the competition for jobs presented by the large number of refugees, particularly those from South Africa.

There is also a large number of European expatriates in Botswana and a small number of Europeans who have taken out citizenship. The latter are periodically criticized for their "paper citizenship"; the former, occupying sensitive technical and policymaking positions, are at times suspected of placing their own national interests above those of Botswana, whether wittingly or not. Finally, the presence of a number of Asian/ Indian businessmen has been a source of increasing tension as their prominence causes some people to believe that they are, or will be, obstacles to Batswana entrepreneurship.

Although the cultural characteristics of these different groups have social and political relevance, it must be remembered that there is heterogeneity within ethnic groups that somewhat mitigates the effect of the cultural differences. However, in important respects, ethnicity coincides with economic position in Botswana, and it is in the economic arena, then, that the primary conflict between ethnic groups occurs. Politically, ethnicity is situational, and one must make a careful analysis of the circumstances under which ethnic factors are politicized, to what extent, in whose interest, and for what reason.

Associations, Group Life, and Culture

A number of associations thrive, including a variety of economic groups such as the Botswana Employers' Federation, local chambers of commerce, farmers associations, the Botswana Civil Servants Association, a range of single-sector industrial unions, and the Botswana Federation of Trade Unions. In addition to providing a point of communication among workers engaged in similar economic functions, these associations operate as interest groups with respect to national and local governments regardless of the ethnicity of the members.

The arts—dance, music, oral history, weaving, and crafts—are an enduring tradition in Botswana. They persist to this day in the fabric of the social life and preserve the indigenous culture. The Botswana

Arts Council, Botswana Society, village groups, and the National Museum are designed to ensure the preservation and growth of this culture.

The independence era has provoked a resurgence of some traditional crafts, and some new techniques have been introduced. The handwoven rugs and wall hangings from Oodi (near Gaborone) and Serowe are recent innovations, and they have become part of a growing export craft industry. Leather working and other crafts have also been introduced or expanded. Traditional basket weaving has become more standardized to produce the volume required for export.

The missionary heritage in Botswana is represented by a substantial Christian population, which is mainly protestant. There is a wide variety of churches, and their activities are coordinated through the Botswana Council of Churches and the Botswana Christian Council. A large proportion of the population practices traditional religion or some combination of that and Christian teachings.

Sports are an important part of social life, the most widespread being football (soccer). League and intravillage/town matches generate considerable interest. Football clubs provide the organizational base, and intense rivalries among clubs exist, sometimes with political overtones. There are sporting-cum-social clubs, mainly for the elite, in the principal towns, such as the Notwane and Gaborone clubs in Gaborone.

Briefly, the sociocultural aspects of contemporary Botswana reveal a multicultural environment with a wide array of activities. They reflect the admixture and adaptations that are to be expected in a newly independent colonial country, and there is a predictable degree of seemingly very different cultures coexisting in one environment.

INSTITUTIONAL CHANGE

A description of political structures involves two aspects. One is the central and local representative, or political institutions, which, under the Constitution, make law and policy and bear responsibility for the actions of the state administrative machinery. The second aspect involves the administrative system of the state in terms of its form, functions, and internal processes.

Political Institutions

Botswana is a parliamentary republic and a unitary state. Its institutions are based on and function according to the Westminster model of parliamentary government, although they incorporate some features of the presidential form of government.

Parliament is the legislative authority and is composed of the president and the National Assembly. The National Assembly consists of thirty-two elected members, four specially elected members, the attorney general, and the Speaker.[2] To date, all specially elected members have been members of the Botswana Democratic party, which has always had an overwhelming majority of elected seats.[3] Qualifications for election to the Assembly are that the person must be a citizen of Botswana, at

The National Assembly.

least twenty-one years of age, registered to vote, and able to speak and "read English well enough to take an active part in the proceedings of the Assembly"[4] which are conducted in English rather than Setswana, which is a national, but not an official government, language.

Subject to certain limitations, Parliament has the power to "make laws for the peace, order, and good government of Botswana," and since independence, the procedure inherent in this power has been adhered to. Members of Parliament engage in active debate and frequently initiate motions, some of which result in government actions.[5] However, the cabinet and the BDP executive do maintain discipline in the Assembly. With one exception,[6] all bills thus far have been introduced by members of the cabinet, and the BDP parliamentary caucus, which meets regularly, provides a means to bring the majority into line. Parliament normally meets three times a year, and the longest session is in March and April when the budget is considered.[7]

Following the Westminster tradition, power resides in Parliament, and the executive is responsible to the legislature. However, the Constitution modifies this relationship by providing for strong presidential powers. Most generally, "the executive power of Botswana shall vest in the President . . . [who shall] act in his own deliberate judgment and shall not be obliged to follow the advice tendered by any other person or authority."[8] Specifically, the president is commander-in-chief of the armed forces; appoints all ministers, assistant ministers, and permanent secretaries; may exercise the prerogative of mercy; and appoints a vice-president. The president's power regarding the National Assembly includes setting the dates and places of meeting, prorogation, and dissolution (subject to a five-year maximum life). The president may withhold assent to any bill; if he does so, it must be returned to the Assembly, and if it again passes, the president must sign it within three weeks or dissolve Parliament. Finally, the Assembly may not proceed on a bill that increases taxation, or expenditures, or alters the composition or remission of government debts unless that bill has been recommended by the president.

Unlike Britain's prime minister, then, the president is more than the primus inter pares with regard to the Assembly and the cabinet. The cabinet—which consists of the president, vice-president, and ministers—is responsible for "advising the President with respect to the policy of the Government," and with some exceptions, the president must "so far as practicable . . . consult the Cabinet on matters of policy and the exercise of his functions."[9]

Once appointed, ministers are individually responsible, "under the direction of the President, for such business of the Government of Botswana (including the administration of any department of Government) as the President may assign to him." However, in parliamentary fashion, the cabinet is collectively "responsible to the National Assembly for all things done by or under the authority of the President, Vice-President or any Minister in the execution of his office."[10]

National judicial authority is organized through the High Court, sitting in Lobatse, and a series of circuit courts throughout the country. Magistrates courts are used in some cases, and minor judicial authority is exercised by the chiefs in customary courts and by district commissioners.

The House of Chiefs is composed of the chiefs of the eight principal tribes, four elected members, and three specially elected members.[11] All bills dealing with the designation, recognition, removal, and powers of chiefs, subchiefs, and headmen or the organization, process, or administration of African courts, African customary law, and tribal organization or property must be referred to the House of Chiefs for discussion. In addition, this body may discuss any matter "of which it considers it is desirable to take cognizance in the interests of the tribes and tribal organizations it represents."[12] The House of Chiefs is, however, an advisory body only. It may discuss bills and issues and may submit its views to Parliament, but those views may or may not influence the final outcome.[13]

Local political institutions include nine district and four town councils, all established by parliament. Their composition includes elected, ex-officio, and nominated members, and they vary in size.[14] The mandated functions of these councils include collecting the local government tax, providing primary education, and carrying out local licensing functions. Their permissive functions are wider, but with limited finances, most have not been in a position to broaden their role. District councils also have a relationship to the land boards, which allocate land use, and to development planning and implementation. They also work with village and district development committees and central government officers in formulating and executing district development plans. Finally, local-level institutions include the traditional authorities, particularly the chiefs, their advisers, staffs, and subordinate headmen. Operating through the *kgotla*, the headmen and chiefs exercise minor, although important, political and judicial functions.

The interrelationship of these national and subnational institutions makes up the formal political process. However, any description of that process must also include the nature of and changes in the administrative apparatus since independence, the dominant features of which have been expansion, specialization, and centralization.

Administrative Institutions

The administrative structure of the state was exceedingly modest at independence, and its functions were still largely administrative (tax collection and the administration of justice) rather than developmental (building infrastructure, education, and production). There were seven ministries plus the Office of the President, the attorney general, the Public Service Commission, and the National Development Bank. In addition, of the 802 senior and middle management positions in 1964, 20 percent were vacant, and more than 75 percent of the occupied positions were held by expatriates. Expatriates even filled 20 percent of the clerical and secretarial positions.[15]

In the first decade of independence, from about 1966/1967 to about 1977/1978, there were dramatic changes in the structure and function of the administrative system. Twenty-six new major institutions were created as well as a number of limited-function ministries, including the Ministries of Finance and Development Planning (1970/1971), Local Government and Lands (1967/1968), Education (1969/1970), Health (1975/1976), and Commerce and Industry and Mineral Resources and Water Affairs (both in 1973/1974). Expansion and specialization also took place on the department level. An Auditor General's Department was created in 1969/1970, and the Departments of Income Tax (1968/1969), Customs and Excise (1971/1972), and Central Transport Organization (1971/1972) are other examples of this expansion.

The number of government-owned commercial type of institutions (parastatals) also increased. In 1966/1967, the only parastatal institution of note was the National Development Bank, a modest successor to the Agricultural Loan Fund. Beginning in 1970/1971, a number of new institutions were created in rapid succession, including the Water Utilities Corporation, Botswana Power Corporation, and Botswana Development Corporation in that year; the Botswana Housing Corporation (1971/1972); the Botswana Livestock Development Corporation (1972/1973); the Botswana Agricultural Marketing Board (1974/1975); and the Bank of Botswana (1975/1976).[16]

All of this proliferation and specialization entailed a drastic expansion of personnel in the public sector, and public sector employment grew rapidly: reaching 13,550 in 1972, increasing to 21,675 in 1976, and constituting 28.3 percent of total employment in 1972 and 30.4 percent in 1976.[17] The number of central government public service posts grew to 1,238 in 1972 and more than doubled to 2,611 in 1977. This growth continued so that total government employment, including education, reached 30,800 in 1980 (or 36.9 percent of all recorded employment).[18]

This institutional and personnel expansion, proliferation, and specialization was both a cause and an effect of greatly expanded and specialized functional activities of the state. The identification of needs in education, infrastructure, and services—particularly to facilitate a development strategy based on a mineral-led economy—caused the creation of a new range of bureaucratic and parastatal institutions. The expansion also represented a more thorough penetration of society by the state, which reflected a new and increased range of resources. The details of this functional change have had a great deal to do with the evolution of a development strategy and the consequences of resource allocation, subjects that are dealt with in Chapters 4 and 5. What is necessary here is to indicate the contours, and stresses and strains, of the institutional issues that arose. Three topics appear to be most significant in this respect: localization, central-local government relations, and interbureau relations.

Localization. The idea of staffing administrative institutions with citizens of Botswana, localization, is a multidimensional issue. One dimension is the extent to which a large expatriate presence introduces or reinforces external influences and control over national policy. Even if these consequences are not automatic, the question arises of how well expatriates can function in appropriate ways; equally important is the issue of what kind of local officer is appropriate. What educational policies and manpower allocations will produce what kinds of citizen officers? Tackling these issues occupies much time and institutional energy in Botswana.

The dramatic increases in the number of people in the public service brought with it an increased number of expatriates. Indeed, by 1977, there were more than twice as many expatriates serving as public officials as there were officials in 1964. In 1972, expatriates filled 41 percent of all posts, a proportion that dropped only marginally to 38 percent in 1977. Even so, the number of vacancies unfilled by either citizens or expatriates remained high, actually increasing from 28 percent in 1972 to 33 percent in 1977.[19]

There has also been concern about the concentration of expatriates in policymaking positions. Nearly 70 percent of the expatriate officials in 1977 were in the technical or professional cadres and therefore critical for policy formulation and execution. Although the very top administrative positions (e.g., the permanent secretary) were largely filled by Botswana citizens (i.e., localized), more than half (59 percent) of the citizen officers were in the executive cadre and therefore not in policymaking positions.[20] This pattern has persisted. In July 1981, 30 percent of the top administrative, 55 percent of the professional, and 35 percent of the senior technical positions were filled by noncitizens.[21]

As a result of concern about this situation,[22] there has been a considerable effort to promote localization. Institutionally, this effort took the form of creating a Directorate of Personnel in 1970 with statutory authority "for training policy, recruitment, promotion and localisation."[23] This directorate took over many of the functions of the more passive Public Service Commission, which retained appellate functions in disciplinary cases. Further supervision of the localization policy has been effected through commissions appointed by the president.

A primary means of achieving localization outside the promotion system has been through educational planning, which has mainly meant the awarding of scholarships and the funding of university-level programs that are specifically directed toward localization concerns. Although these methods have produced quantities of formally qualified officers, they have also resulted in restrictions of student choice, limitations on the diversity of programs offered, and a uniformity in the kind of public officials that results.

Central-Local Government Relations. The second issue area is that of central-local relations, which has two related dimensions. One is the relationship between traditional authorities and elected/bureaucratic officials; the second is the hierarchical relationship between central/national and local governments.

In its 1965 election manifesto, the BDP committed itself to a "*gradual* but *sure* evolution of a national state in Bechuanaland, to which tribal groups will, while they remain in existence, take a secondary place. This is an unavoidable development, an evolutionary law to which we must yield to survive, or resist and disappear as a people."[24] The cultural identity of the various ethnic groups and the colonial history of the chiefs' powers were viewed by the new elite as obstructive in the long run. At the same time, it was recognized that the ethnic unit and the chiefs continued to be politically important for the majority of the people, the peasantariat. Hence, in the late colonial and early postcolonial periods, there was a gradual, but sure, diminishing of the power of the traditional authorities, although they continue to exist and perform essential political functions.[25]

The first step toward this diminishing of power was the creation of elected district councils in 1966. At this point, chiefs were not excluded from the councils—indeed, they were initially ex-officio chairpersons—but at the same time, the Chieftainship Act of 1965 vested the powers of recognition, appointment, deposition, and suspension of chiefs in the president. The act also confirmed many of the chiefs' existing powers, including their functions in customary courts; their power to seize stolen property and collect and sell *matimela* (stray cattle); their authority in the regulation of tribal affairs; their right to convene meetings of the *kgotla*; and, finally, their power to allocate land for agricultural and other uses.

In subsequent years, many of these powers were either removed or chiefs were required to share them with the elected councils and/ or the central government. In 1970, the allocation of land became a tripartite responsibility of the chiefs, councils, and central government.[26] The chiefs' right to age-group (regiment) labor for public works was removed, and the district councils assumed the right to impound and sell stray cattle. The right to tax revenue and many judicial functions were altered, and most of the staff and administrative assets of the chiefs were transferred to the councils. Chiefs were removed as ex-officio chairpersons of the councils, although they retained their seats and eligibility for election as chairperson. The only increase in the power of chiefs was the authority to impose sentences of up to four years or a fine up to P 4,000 in cases of stock theft. The continued existence of the position of chief recognizes the important symbolic function they perform, but beyond this largely ideological role, the traditional authorities have been more or less removed from the policymaking and administrative structures.

The increased power of the district councils, gained at the expense of the traditional authorities, highlighted the need for clearly developed policies and authority guidelines for the central and local governments. The issues involved the appropriate role of local decision making in the national context, the perception of the relative weakness of local personnel to manage resources, and, finally, the extent to which national development policies could be coordinated when there were semiautonomous local governments. From independence to about 1970, the dominant trend was toward decentralization. From about 1971 to 1980, there was a trend toward greater central government control, and since 1980, new relationships have been developing.

Decentralization meant that the semiautonomous district councils exercised their powers under the Local Government Act. Central government officers worked alongside local government officials in the districts, and the district commissioners, as the representative of the Ministry of Local Government and Lands (MLGL), sought to supervise and coordinate activities but had only a little authority to do so. Councils employed their own staffs and sought to develop as viable institutions of government.

Two main problems arose. First, the councils relied on a local government tax, essentially a regressive tax that hit the poor most heavily, which was unpopular, difficult and expensive to collect, and impossible to increase. Increasingly, the councils began to rely more and more on central government grants, which meant that the central government felt responsible for seeing that the money was spent properly.[27] Second, the councils found it difficult to attract well-qualified staffs. The central government could outbid them in terms of salaries and opportunities for advancement; hence, the ability of the councils to attract and retain suitable staffs was limited.

Beginning in 1970, the relationship moved in the direction of greater central government supervision and control of district councils while allowing some decision making and implementation of development projects on the local level. The new land boards, for example, had central government representatives. In addition, in 1970, the district councils act was amended to stipulate that the district commissioners would be ex-officio members, with the right to examine the books of the councils, and that they would receive and inspect all documents of the councils.[28] In 1975, an amendment to the Tribal Land Act gave the president the power to alter any decision of any land board, and in the same year, the minister of commerce and industry was given the power to limit the number of trading licenses that could be issued to an individual—a power that was related to the councils' responsibilities under the Trading Act.[29]

New policies in 1971 also had the effect of creating a more coherent and a more powerful central government presence in the districts. A presidential circular in late 1970 stipulated that "in each District, the District Commissioner is the principal representative of Government on political and policy matters," and he is responsible for coordinating government activities and "responsible for the efficient conduct of public business."[30] District development committees, chaired by the district commissioner and composed of central government representatives in the district along with invited members, were created to manage the central government's new responsibilities. The post of district officer development was created—staffed mainly by volunteer expatriates—to provide assistance to the district commissioner and to act as secretary of the development committee.[31] In the late 1970s, a new post of district officer (lands) was created to assist the land board and the district commissioner in implementing the tribal grazing lands policy.

Finally, the central government sought to attack the manpower problem of the councils by creating the Unified Local Government Service in 1973. Henceforth, district council administrative staffs would be recruited and appointed centrally on terms and conditions of service that were equivalent to their public service counterparts. Although this policy made service in local government more attractive, it also loosened the autonomy of the district councils by decreasing their control over their staffs.[32]

These developments are noteworthy in three respects. One, power and administrative authority have shifted from the traditional authorities to the councils without eliminating the former entirely. Second, there has been a shift from a more independent council system to one in which the central government plays an increasingly strong role. But, third, the central government has not sought to eliminate what might be seen as an unnecessary duplication of local and central government institutions. Indeed, the central government has protected the continued existence of the councils and, in some respects, has asked them to become more responsible and effective units.[33]

The stresses and strains of the 1970s generated ideas in the early 1980s for a new, hybridized, local government system. The 1979 Presidential Commission on Local Government Structure recognized the political and administrative desirability of strong local institutions, but it also recognized that council and tribal personnel and financial problems required central government involvement and supervision. The commission argued that viable local government required, one, that "districts must be allocated a higher proportion of national resources—finance, and above all, top calibre manpower" and, two, that the central government must decentralize more effectively.[34] It also argued that chiefs should become the central ceremonial head of each district and that their staffs should serve in the Unified Local Government Service. At the same time, central government supervision should be strengthened by the appointment of a district development director, a sort of super district commissioner, who would be shorn of magisterial and routine functions. These changes, in the commission's view, would give new coherence and strength to local government.

However, no major restructuring of local government took place in the early 1980s; instead, attention was focused on the manpower problem on the local level. Consultants viewed this problem as primary, arguing that the situation was so serious that "it verges on being catastrophic in the next few years" and estimating a total training need of 5,649 people between 1982 and 1992.[35] However, the issues of a appropriate role for local government and the relationship between central and local governments remained.

Interbureau Relations. This fluidity of central-local relations is a good illustration of the final issue of institutional evolution, namely, that of institutions' differing views about their roles. Such competing views were largely brought about by the proliferation of institutions after independence as the creation of specialized ministries and parastatals generated new institutional and bureaucratic interests. A certain level of interministerial competition has therefore marked the period from 1970 to the present.[36]

This competition may be illustrated by national-level ministries. A certain amount of conflict has taken place between the functional institutions (e.g., Works and Communications, Education, Health) and the process ones (e.g., the Office of the President and the Ministry of Finance and Development Planning). Another example would be the conflict between the MLGL and other ministries concerning the appropriate role of local government and its supervision. The "senior" ministries (the Office of the President and the Ministry of Finance and Development Planning) have emerged as the most powerful institutions, but the differing views of what should be done and by whom still provides an underlying base of bureaucratic conflict.

Thus, in the contemporary period, political and administrative institutions have proliferated, expanded, and specialized, and these changes have provoked issues concerning collective institutions. It should be remembered, however, that these institutional changes and debates have not taken place independently of the nature of and the changes in the social and political environment of which they are part.

POSTCOLONIAL POLITICAL DEVELOPMENT

The most striking postcolonial political phenomenon in Botswana has been the stability and continuity of the political landscape. Transplanted political institutions, which lack historical legitimacy and which—in certain socioeconomic circumstances—have resulted in significant upheavals elsewhere, have survived and apparently thrived. In an environment of relative political tolerance, multiparty politics have endured, although one party is dominant. This political stability has survived in spite of the death of Seretse Khama, whose singular role was often cited as a primary factor in this continuity.

Describing and explaining the political situation is an important task and adds to the description of contemporary Botswana. The task can be partially accomplished by first surveying the electoral situation, then describing the Botswana Democratic party and its organized opposition, and finally outlining the succession issue.

The BDP Predominant: Elections and Parties 1969-1979

Botswana has had three postindependence general elections. All three have involved multiple political parties, and in all three, the Botswana Democratic party (BDP) has won handsomely. Indeed, if anything, the BDP has increased its hold on elected positions.

Table 3.1 presents illustrative data on National Assembly elections. The BDP is the only party that has fielded candidates for all seats, and it has increased its number of seats won from 24 in 1969 to 27 in 1974 to 29 in 1979. The combined opposition won only 7 seats in 1969 and only 3 in 1979. Although there has been drastic change in the number of votes cast from one election to another, the BDP has consistently won an overwhelming plurality, capturing 68.6 percent of the total votes in 1969, 76.6 percent in 1974, and 75.2 percent in 1979. Voter turnout has varied, but in situations of both low turnout (1974) and higher turnout (1979), the BDP has garnered more than three-quarters of the votes cast.

District and town council elections have followed a similar pattern, although the geographical bases of the two opposition parties have meant that for a few councils, opposition majorities have been elected.[37] In 1969, the BDP won 113 of 165 elected seats in local government elections. It lost to the Botswana Peoples' party in the Francistown and North East District Council elections and finished even with the Botswana National Front in Lobatse and Gaborone. In 1974, the BDP won 149 of 176 elected seats, and only the North East District Council had an elected majority of opposition members. In 1979, the BDP won 147 of 176 seats, including elected majorities on all councils.[38]

Parties and Politics

The BDP has been, therefore, highly successful as an electoral and a governing party. Before reaching the conclusion that the BDP is as

TABLE 3.1
National Assembly Elections by Year and Party

Year and Election Variable		Party			
		BDP	BIP	BNF	BPP
Seats contested as	1969	100%	29.0%	67.7%	48.4%
% of total seats	1974	100	18.8	43.8	25.0
	1979	100	15.6	50.0	43.8
Seats won	1969	24	1	3	3
	1974	27	1	2	2
	1979	29	0	2	1
Number of votes[a]	1969	52,518	4,601	10,410	9,329
	1974	49,047	3,086	7,358	4,199
	1979	101,098	5,657	17,480	9,983
% Share of total	1969	68.3%	6.0%	13.5%	12.1%
vote	1974	76.6	4.8	11.5	6.6
	1979	75.3	4.2	13.0	7.4
National turnout	1969		54.7%		
(votes cast as %	1974		31.2		
of eligible voters)	1979		58.4		

[a] The number of votes cast excludes votes for independent
candidates. Votes for independent candidates totaled 321 in 1974
and 278 in 1979. No such votes were recorded in 1969.

Sources: W.J.A. Macartney, "The General Election of 1969,"
Botswana Notes and Records 3 (1971), pp. 32-37; Supervisor of
Elections, Report on the General Elections 1969 (Gaborone:
Government Printer, 1970); Supervisor of Elections, Report to the
Minister of State on the General Elections, 1974 (Gaborone:
Government Printer, n.d.); Supervisor of Elections, Report to the
Minister of Public Service and Information on the General
Election, 1979 (Gaborone: Government Printer, n.d.).

popular as the figures would indicate, it is necessary to place electoral
outcomes in their political context. Essentially, the success of the BDP
must be seen in relation to its structure, activities, social base, and the
context of growth and change in Botswana.

   The Botswana Democratic Party: The Politics of Success and the Success
of Politics. The constitution of the BDP creates a mass-based structure.
Cells, subwards, wards, subbranches, constituency branches, regional
organizations, the national congress, council, and central committee
constitute the hierarchy of the party.[39] There is also a youth wing. The
party's physical manifestation consists of party officials, district offices,

A political rally in Molepolole, 1974.

and the edifice of Tsholetsa House in Gaborone, national party head-quarters. Tsholetsa House is the headquarters for the executive secretary and a small supporting staff.

This formal mass structure, however, masks the more informal nature of the party. The BDP operates more as a cadre than a mass party, and in the districts, especially between elections, the party is highly dependent on the personalities of the constituency's member of Parliament and other local notables. On the national level, the party operates as a congenial coalition of these district notables combined with a bureaucratic political elite.

The party is supported financially by dues and especially by voluntary contributions, the latter presumably from the business community and the party's main supporters who have incomes derived from salaries and agricultural pursuits. In addition, the bulk of the office space in Tsholetsa House is rented to government departments and small businesses, which yields additional income.[40]

Between elections, the party organization is more or less dormant, and its district and constituency organizations are relatively inactive. Meetings of the party's national council and central committee, the BDP caucus of members of Parliament, and the annual congress are the primary activities. At the time of a general election, however, the BDP becomes a well-oiled and financed machine. In 1974, for example, the BDP hired fifty organizers; bought twenty-two bicycles, twelve new motor vehicles, and twenty-four loudspeaker systems; mounted a two-week course on campaigning for twenty-four people; held regional

Tsholetsa House, headquarters of the Botswana Democratic party.

seminars; produced material on campaigning; paid for the printing of 35,000 copies of the party's manifesto and thousands of posters; and paid part of the expenses of the party's candidates.[41] In the words of one participant, the BDP "went to the election like a teacher who has thoroughly done his preparations."[42] With this level of activity, it is clear that "opposing the Domkrag giant is . . . a daunting task,"[43] and no doubt this level of resources and activity is critical to the party's electoral success. Just after the 1974 election, however, the vehicles were sold, the loudspeakers stored, and staff laid off until needed again. The pattern in 1979 was similar.

The BDP's electoral success continues to be based on peasantariat support, and the party leaders' socioeconomic status also continues to distinguish them from the mass base. In 1969, for example, John Holm found that although 20 percent of the general population claimed some form of traditional status, "50% of the MP's sampled and 60% of the councillors said that their families had paternal kinship ties with a local chief or headman." Although 90 percent of the population had had no more than three years of education, all members of Parliament and 70 percent of the councillors had had this experience. In addition, the majority of the parliamentary members and councillors were substantial cattleowners and/or arable farmers and/or small businessmen.[44] Data from 1974[45] confirm Holm's views as then, too, members of the National Assembly and councillors had significantly more education, higher traditional status, and a better economic position than the mass of the population.

Those facts do not mean that either the party elite or mass represents a homogeneous entity or that the ties that bind are purely artificial and symbolic. Indeed, the party mass and elite are diverse, and the ties between them are material as well as ideological.

The BDP elite on the district level, for example, is less educated than the elite on the national level. The district elites also tend to have a smaller bureaucratic element and are largely drawn from the *dikgosana* (people of traditional status who are related to royalty). Their interests are centered more on the local economy and scene instead of cross-district or national affairs. The national elite is closer to the central decision making, and its future is very much bound up with national policy. There is, therefore, some scope for conflict within the BDP elite.

The mass base of the BDP is also diverse. It includes a range of ethnic groups, although it is centered on a common Tswana identity. In addition, some members are engaged in manual work, in and outside of Botswana, and/or in agriculture, which creates distinct political positions and outlooks.

The common bond of the BDP elite and the mass electoral base is based on a combination of material and ideological factors. Its ideological content centers on the traditional economic, social, and political orders that were formed by the colonial system and is implicit in the structure of the BDP. The prevalence of party members of high ethnic and traditional status and the association of the BDP with the maintenance of traditional authority provide a legitimacy that is not easily undermined.

Materially, the bond is maintained in two primary ways. One is the relationships between people involved in agriculture, primarily those that bind the cattleowner to the noncattleowner. Loans and various forms of employment are conditions that make the noncattleowner dependent on those who control the means of production. As long as the peasantariat has access to loaned cattle, the relationship appears to be not only one of dependence but more, a relationship of mutual interest and benefit. The members of the peasantariat are therefore likely to feel a positive bond with their patrons, many of whom also have traditional political status and are local leaders or supporters of the BDP. At election time, such relationships translate into votes for the BDP. This economic and political relationship has thus far hindered the development of a political organization that would represent the peasantariat directly. Such a development is also prevented by the peasantariat's lack of education or organizational skills, internal divisions, and geographical dispersal.[46]

Second, the BDP has enjoyed the status of being the incumbent party during a time of expanding resources and services as the period since independence has been a period of real and dramatic, if uneven, growth. The fact that the benefits of this growth may be very unequally distributed is masked for many people by the small but real benefits that have been made widely available. "The BDP government has been able to spend its way out of political trouble."[47] The most obvious case is the Accelerated Rural Development Programme, which was put in operation at the time of the 1974 election. More generally, the growth associated with the postindependence era has reflected favorably on the BDP, as it would on any incumbent that takes credit for achievements.

These relationships and this allocation of resources mean that the BDP's mass base has been secure. The extent to which that connection can be and is being maintained has a great deal to do with any analysis of Botswana's development strategy and its consequences, but it also has to do with the nature and activity of the opposition parties.

The "Chink in the Armor": The Organized Opposition. None of the three opposition political parties has presented a serious threat to the BDP's hold on government—which, of course, is one possible explanation for the maintenance and stability of multiparty politics in Botswana. All three opposition parties depend on regional/ethnic bases of support for their minimal success, despite efforts by one party in particular to develop a more national organization. None of the opposition parties comes even close to the BDP in the quantity and quality of organization, finance, and manpower.

However, the persistence of opposition parties indicates that there are parts of the country and a political elite that have not been beguiled by the siren song of successful incumbency. That observation alone is a good reason to examine, if only briefly, the structures and activities of the organized opposition parties.

The BPP and BIP: Grim Determination. The Botswana Peoples' party (BPP) and the Botswana Independence party (BIP) have seen their fortunes decline in the postindependence era. Both have been dominated by particular personalities and rely upon ethnic or regional support.

The BPP, it will be recalled, was the first real political party to be formed in Bechuanaland. Leadership splits and a lack of resources and organizers meant that at independence, the BPP had only a regional base in the northeastern part of the country and the urban area of Francistown. The party appealed to many Kalanga people and others who felt that the BDP was dominated by a self-aggrandizing Tswana elite. Some people felt that this elite ignored the needs of non-Tswana people and the particular problems of the land-hungry northeastern part of the country, an area that has supported the BPP in National Assembly and district council elections.

In the 1974 elections, the BPP fielded eight candidates and captured 6.6 percent of the vote and two seats, in the North East District and Francistown (the latter won by the party leader, P. G. Matante). These results compared with the party's 1969 performance when it presented fifteen candidates, garnered 12.1 percent of the votes, and won three seats. In 1979, despite increasing its number of candidates to fourteen and marginally increasing its share of the vote in comparison to 1974, the party won only one seat—P. G. Matante losing to the former executive secretary of the BDP in Francistown.[48]

The BPP has not built a permanent party organization. Its last party document was issued in 1967, and its organization appears to rest now almost entirely on narrow sectional, although real, appeal. The death of Matante in late 1979 undoubtedly weakened the party's appeal and viability even further.

A polling place in Molepolole, 1974, displaying the symbols of the BDP and the BNF.

The organization, activities, and decline of the Botswana Independence party parallel those of the BPP. Most highly organized in the Okavango constituency and drawing on an ethnic/regional base centered on the Bayei of that area, the BIP is increasingly the party of Motsamai Mpho. Although the party sponsored nine candidates and won 6 percent of the votes and one seat in 1969, in 1979, the party fielded only five candidates and won only 4.2 percent of the vote and no seats—Mpho even lost in his own constituency by a substantial majority.[49] Hence, the BIP has become a very marginal party, even in its home territory, despite the considerable organizational skills and political acumen of its founder and leader.

The Botswana National Front (BNF). Of the three opposition parties, the BNF remains the most viable. However, it represents an uneasy combination of traditionalism and a type of socialist rhetoric, has only a regional base, lacks sufficient resources and organization, and has been no more successful than the other opposition parties in challenging the BDP.

Founded shortly after the 1965 election by Kenneth Koma, the BNF opposed what it saw as the BDP "marriage of convenience between archaic tribal feudalism and the emergent bureaucratic bourgeoisie on the one hand and neo-colonialism on the other hand." It saw the task as being one of organizing a "national democratic struggle" led by the "radical section of the middle class" in the long-term interests of the proletariat. The short-term tactic to achieve this aim would be to form alliances with the corrupt feudal elements, the chiefs. This tactic was necessary because of the nature of the workers' support—"when we speak of a worker . . . we are speaking of a peasant worker with immediate tribal connections."[50]

Koma's strategy bore some fruit as the party was able to form a coalition with Bathoen Gaseitsiwe, chief of the Bangwaketse in southern Botswana. He resigned his position to engage in politics in opposition to the BDP's determination to remove the chiefs from a central political role, and he presumably saw the BNF as a means of support. Bathoen was president of the BNF until 1977 when Koma succeeded him.

Bathoen brought an electoral base to the BNF, although it was largely ethnic. In 1969, the BNF sponsored twenty-one National Assembly candidates, attracted 13.5 percent of votes, and won three seats, all within the ethnic/regional base contributed by Bathoen.[51] Although the BNF captured half the seats on the Lobatse and Gaborone town councils, demonstrating some urban appeal, its main strength on the local level was represented by its winning eleven of twenty-four elected seats on the Southern District Council.

In 1974, the BNF attempted to mobilize urban working-class discontent, attract the support of disgruntled middle-level civil servants, and secure peasantariat support through Bathoen. As it turned out, the BNF sponsored only fourteen candidates, and its proportion of the votes declined to 11.5 percent. Kenneth Koma lost badly in Gaborone, attracting less than half the votes against W. Seboni, the incumbent BDP member of Parliament and ex-mayor. Quett Masire won the Ngwaketse/Kgalagadi seat for the BDP, and the BNF won only the Kanye North and Kanye South seats. In local elections, the BNF won ten seats on the Southern District Council and only two seats elsewhere.[52]

Between 1974 and 1979, the BNF attempted to reorganize and remain active. It was the only opposition party to regularly hold rallies outside its regional base and to regularly hold meetings in "freedom squares," particularly in Gaborone. Koma assumed the party's presidency, reissued party documents, and declared that the party would perform well in 1979 and aim at winning outright in the 1984 election.[53] However, in 1979, the BNF fielded only sixteen candidates. Its proportion of the vote rose marginally to 13 percent, but it still managed to win only the two Kanye seats. The party was still bedeviled by an ethnic base and had yet to demonstrate an appeal based on other factors.[54]

The BNF did not solve its problems, or build a more successful base, in the early 1980s. It continues to be the most vocal opposition party, commenting on and criticizing BDP policies, but by doing so, it also continues to be a primary political target of the BDP and often draws the verbal fire of senior BDP members.[55] Although the BNF will be a factor in future elections, there is little likelihood, given its history and circumstances, that it will be an electoral threat.

Succession: Continuity and Change in the Botswana Polity

Until his death in 1980, Seretse Khama occupied a central political position. The creation of a dominant and pervasive set of national government institutions was highly dependent on his status as a traditional leader who went beyond a narrow regional or ethnic base. He materialized the ideological connection between the governing elite and the mass peasantariat base. He was also the focal point of the otherwise uneasy coalition of senior bureaucrats and the socioeconomic group that governed through the BDP. Seretse Khama moved easily between these apparently contradictory groups.

Enormous changes in the social, political, and economic infrastructure have taken place during the postcolonial period. The proliferation of education and other government services have opened opportunities that were unknown before, and the widening of the elite has brought new and somewhat unpredictable sociopolitical elements into play. Economic growth has generated the utilization of large resources and opportunities that have begun to restructure the economy of the country.

The management of the resulting political stresses has been successful largely because of Seretse Khama and the legitimacy he created for the whole process. Because of his importance and the fact that there was no successor who had similar attributes, there was considerable speculation during Khama's lifetime about his successor. Would stability outlive its instigator? The answer is not entirely certain, but the succession to date has been quiet and successful. Masire assumed the presidency immediately after Khama's death and was subsequently elected to that post by the National Assembly.

President Masire brought an impressive set of credentials to his new office. He was a founder of the BDP and played a leadership role from the beginning. He was selected by Khama to be vice-president at the beginning of the postindependence period, and in addition, he was minister of finance and development planning, a pivotal position, until he became president. Since Masire had been a prime architect of the development strategy, there was no policy discontinuity to be resolved. In addition, his leadership of the ministry had made him knowledgeable about virtually all areas of the public sector and the economy at large. In terms of institutional experience, Masire was prepared for the new job.

Masire, however, also has two political liabilities. First, before becoming president, he lived in Khama's shadow and did not have a clearly independent position in the elite, and a long-term successful succession depends in part upon his being able to develop a base in that elite. More important, Masire does not have the automatic legitimacy that was accorded Seretse Khama because of his traditional status. This fact potentially limits Masire's ability to maintain a cohesive leadership group and to trigger automatic peasantariat support. For both of these reasons, there is at least more uncertainty about the wielding of power at the center than there was during Khama's presidency.

There has been substantial continuity in Botswana in the postindependence period. That continuity indicates the strength of the governing elite and its connections with a mass base; it also indicates the country's very good luck in having diamonds discovered there as well as considerable skill in adjusting to the international environment.

However, enough has also been said to indicate that the political situation in contemporary Botswana is not without its contradictions and tensions. The primary stresses concern the elite's control of resources and the problems inherent in developing the country without upsetting the mass base. A great deal also depends on how much further economic growth alleviates the great inequalities that were generated by or have expanded since independence. It is in these critical areas that the elite's development strategy and the consequences of its implementation are important, topics that are addressed in the following two chapters.

4

Development Strategy: Rationale

The creation of new institutions and relationships, the undertaking of new and redefinitions of old economic activities, and the sociocultural phenomena that resulted, intended and unintended, define the contemporary period. These were not random events; they were part of a planned attempt to change.

The design of development is primarily a political act. There are, of course, narrow economic choices to be made as no politician or consultant can simply will the necessary resources and infrastructure into being. But strategies and projects, and their implementation, are primarily political actions because they concern the generation and distribution of resources, socioeconomic relations, and income and the use of state power to carry out the plans decided upon. No amount of technical formulas or expertise removes that fundamental fact of life. Development is, therefore, a process that is closely related to the interests of the people who design it and unevenly and unequally affects those people who experience its consequences.

POLITICAL ECONOMY OF BOTSWANA ABOUT 1966

At independence, the political economy of Botswana was that of a labor reserve country, and it was within that context that late colonial development took place and postcolonial planning evolved. It is therefore necessary to review the state of that economy at independence in order to understand the specific nature of the sequence and content of the development planning that followed.

Botswana's economy was weak in 1966, and important elements of it were extensions of external economies rather than independent national sectors. For example, the primary transportation system, the railway, was an extension of Rhodesia's railway system; the country's roads were an extension of South Africa's, and they were primarily used to channel labor to South Africa and distribute commodities produced there; and Botswana's agriculture, manufacturing, and trade were primarily determined by the country's place in the South African orbit, as illustrated by the Southern African Customs Union and the Rand Monetary Area. There were no areas of public service that could be said to be quantitatively or qualitatively adequate, and this absolute inadequacy of Botswana's economy was most dramatically illustrated in the final colonial years by the country's reliance on the British Exchequer for the financing of the government's small recurrent budget.[1]

The level of underdevelopment at the time may be indicated by a range of data. The gross domestic product (GDP) in 1966 was P 36.9 million, of which agriculture, forestry, hunting, and fishing accounted for P 11.1 million, or 30 percent; mining, manufacturing, water and electricity generation, and building and other construction combined accounted for only 19 percent; wholesale and retail trade, restaurants, and hotels accounted for 13.7 percent. Imports of goods amounted to 57 percent of GDP; exports of goods represented 32.8 percent. It was an externally oriented, low-productivity, and relatively undifferentiated economy.[2]

These features of the economy were reproduced and reflected in the level of available social services and amenities. There were few all-weather roads, and education was provided only at the primary level and only for a small proportion of the population. In 1967, there were 71,577 pupils in primary schools with a teacher-pupil ratio of 1:42, and 38 percent of the teachers were untrained.[3] Secondary education for a very select group was available in South Africa, and higher education was available to a small number in Lesotho and abroad. In 1963, there were only 45 Batswana in institutions of higher education.[4]

The population, estimated at 528,955 in 1964, was young and rural. Only 3.9 percent lived in urban areas, and more than one-third lived in settlements of 1,000 to 4,999.[5] The livelihood of more than 90 percent of the population depended upon the underdeveloped rural economy, but that economy could not support the population. A 1967/1968 agricultural survey conservatively estimated that 10 percent of the whole population had no visible means of support at all.[6]

There were few opportunities to work in Bechuanaland itself. It was estimated in 1965 that of a labor force that totaled 251,000, only 12 percent was recorded as being paid for work or services performed in urban and rural areas of the country.[7] In 1964, a total of 13,850 people were recorded as being employed in Bechuanaland, and nearly half of them were employed by the government.[8]

Therefore, large numbers of people had to leave the country to earn a livelihood. The absentee population in 1964 was conservatively estimated at 30,476,[9] and it increased to 42,000 in 1968.[10] Of the active labor force in 1964—people between the ages of fifteen and fifty years— slightly more than one-fifth of all males and about 5 percent of the females were employed outside the country. In the age group of twenty to thirty-five, these proportions were just over one-third of all males and about 6 percent of females.[11]

South African labor recruiting compound in Molepolole.

This absent labor force reflected and caused low productivity in agriculture, the main sector of the economy. The lack of a well-developed infrastructure was important, but so, too, was the withdrawal of a large proportion of the available labor force, primarily male, from agricultural production. Yet the national economy had to provide subsistence for a very young population, and this fact continued to drive people into becoming migrant laborers. The overall result was widespread poverty: In 1970, the estimated rural per capita income was only about P 35 per annum.[12]

Some social aspects of agricultural production contributed to the underdevelopment. The primary agricultural asset was oxen as the ownership of or timely access to oxen was required for arable farming. But cattle were both privately owned and unequally distributed. The 1968/1969 agricultural survey showed that nearly 30 percent of the agricultural holders owned no cattle at all and that nearly 21 percent owned between one and ten. Nearly 75 percent of all agricultural holders owned twenty-five or fewer cattle. At the other end of the spectrum, 12 percent of the holders had fifty-one or more cows, accounting for 59 percent of all the cattle owned.[13] Nonowners had difficulty producing food, and this fact forced the males into migrant labor. The women then bore the main burden of agricultural production, and they rarely owned or had regular access to oxen. The agricultural system did distribute the use of animals as the small cattle-owning elite relied on peasantariat labor and made some oxen available in return, although not always at the right moment.

The cattle-owning group might have been able to further develop agriculture if it had not been for the system of land tenure. Four percent of the land was freehold (privately owned) and divided into six "blocks," 49 percent of the land was communally owned by the eight tribes, and the remaining 47 percent was state land.[14] Community and state ownership of land, although protecting the peasantariat, limited the ability and the incentive of the large cattleowners to invest in commercial development because exclusive rights over land could not be guaranteed.

Thus, the low productivity of agriculture could not be improved by the peasantariat beause of their lack of draft animals, and intensive commercial farming could not be easily developed because the cattleowners could not control the land. Although the latter group was politically preeminent, there were constraints on its activity.

Botswana's national economy at the time of independence was therefore weak, externally oriented, and underdeveloped. It was primarily characterized by its incorporation into the broader southern African regional economy, which was dominated by South Africa. Class relations reflected this economic base and its history, and opportunities to change these relations were limited. In addition, the natural environment was uncertain as the permanent water supply was limited and rainfall was unpredictable. This was the base on which Botswana had to attempt development.

COLONIAL DEVELOPMENT: 1955–1966

Not surprisingly, development strategy in the late colonial period had something of a desperate quality about it. From the 1950s onward, the imminence of national independence highlighted the stark facts that there was no national economy to go along with independence and there were numerous obstacles to the creation of such an economy.

The late colonial development strategy that emerged was based upon the rather short-term goals of achieving budgetary self-sufficiency in domestic revenue, providing the trappings of national institutions, and beginning to develop an infrastructure that would underpin the commercialization of agriculture. The last goal would be achieved by reforms and services in communal areas, mainly "by opening up new grazing areas for individual African ranchers and syndicates in the Tribal Territories under a loan scheme for water development" and by handing over suitable state land for ranching settlement.[15] The implicit thrust of these plans supported the agricultural interests of an emerging elite in the political parties.

The resulting expenditures represented a "shopping list" of investments on several not closely interrelated fronts. During the 1954/1955 to 1964/1965 period, P 8,536,000 of colonial development and welfare funds were committed. Eighteen percent went for underground water development to open new grazing areas and to alleviate serious drought problems, and only slightly less was spent in developing the educational system. Eleven percent went to build the capital in Gaborone,

The main shopping mall in Gaborone.

and this project accounted for 20 percent of the expenditures in the years after 1960/1961. Twelve percent went into veterinary projects, more than half for control of foot-and-mouth disease. Natural resource surveys absorbed just over 8 percent of the total amount, and public works, particularly road and bridge building, accounted for just under 8 percent. Thus, three-quarters of all expenditures were absorbed by the attempt to generate a minimal infrastructure, alleviate immediate problems, and generate data for planning by the time of independence.[16]

BEGINNINGS OF A NEW DEVELOPMENT STRATEGY: 1966–1970

The new government's initial *Transitional Plan for Social and Economic Development* was an extension of colonial plans and projects. Its time horizons were necessarily short-term and rooted in the immediacy of financial problems and "the necessity of planning the social and economic development of the nation." The most fundamental priority was a "determination to make the country a financially viable entity in the shortest possible period." The means were to be careful planning and a rapid, if incremental, increase in opportunities for work and revenue, which forced the long-range objective of "a more equitable distribution of income" into the background. The resulting shopping list of projects was similar to that under the government's colonial predecessor.[17]

By 1970, the situation began to change as people argued for the formulation of a more consistent and complex strategy. Two developments were particularly important. One was the renegotiation of the Southern African Customs Union Agreement,[18] and although the new agreement did not give Botswana a great deal of control over tariff levels, it did greatly increase government revenues. This increase, along with other developments, allowed the achievement of budgetary self-sufficiency in

1972/1973. Second, the discovery of commercially viable deposits of copper/nickel and diamonds raised the possibility of greatly increased future revenues, investments, and employment opportunities.

The immediate issue dominating the development plan published in late 1970 was how to get the new mines into production. Beyond that problem, the plan described the development strategy only very generally. It presented concepts of social justice, equality of opportunity, and persuasion rather than coercion, and specific economic goals were the "fastest possible rate of economic growth," the achievement of budgetary self-sufficiency, a maximal creation of jobs, and the promotion of "an equitable distribution of income, in particular, by reducing income differentials between the urban and the rural sectors through rural development."[19] Beyond these statements, the plan did not present a coherent strategy in terms of choices to be made. Although it expressed the need for sectoral specification and balanced growth, the job of constructing a development strategy still remained.

FORMULATION OF A STRATEGY: PRINCIPLES AND SPECIFICS, 1970–1980

The process of constructing a development strategy was inexact and fraught with difficulty. For one thing, a large proportion of the planning officers were young and inexperienced expatriates who were literally learning on the job, so mistakes, imprecision, and inadequate judgment were inevitable. Second, so little was known about the availability of resources and the nature of the environment that the data base used for planning had been drawn up with as much conjecture as certitude. Third, national planning was a new activity, and much had to be learned about how the economy and society would respond to initiatives from the central government. Finally, the planning process was somewhat unpredictable because as events unfolded, the planning context was changed or overtaken.

Nonetheless, one can impose an organization and a sequence to Botswana's construction of a development strategy. Two primary areas are discussed: the strategy of a mineral-led growth and the strategy of development resting on mineral revenue, followed by a more comprehensive review of subsidiary, though no less important, matters.

A Mineral-Led Economy

Botswana had the good fortune to discover the existence of significant mineral deposits. No other economic activity in the country could match the revenue-raising potential of mining, and as early as 1970, the development plan noted that the projected rapid development of the economy was "almost entirely dependent on the successful creation of a mining sector."[20]

Although the basic strategy of relying on mining seemed unavoidable, a number of issues had to be confronted. Among these were the rate at which mining could take place, the division of the revenues between private investors and the government, the organization of production, the marketing of the product, and the relationship between the mining industry and secondary and tertiary economic activities.

The formulation of policies in these areas developed over a period of years on the basis of experience. Initially, the government was in a very weak position. It did not have the manpower, assets, or market contacts to develop and operate mines on its own behalf, and the choice of companies with which it could realistically negotiate was limited as South African concerns almost had a monopoly on the technology and organization of mining in the region. Indeed, the 1970–1975 plan contained little guidance about policies regarding mining as the chapter on mining development essentially outlined only the process of developing the copper/nickel mine. As the years passed, and as diamond mining became spectacularly successful, it was possible to drive a harder bargain and to formulate more-specific policies.

Government and Foreign Investment: The Division of Responsibility

Botswana welcomed foreign investment as the means to overcome the problems of scarcities of manpower and capital. To attract investment, the government promised to maintain "a suitable investment climate" and offer a "range of specific financial incentives" under the general umbrella of allowing investors a "fair return" on their investment. The former included constitutional guarantees against expropriation without compensation,[21] and further, the government undertook to control exchange policy to "permit the transfer of profits and dividends to countries outside Botswana without undue restriction."[22] In addition, financial incentives could be negotiated in individual cases. These might include favorable tax packages, generous write-off provisions, or a range of allowances depending upon the specific foreign investment.[23]

The role of foreign mining investment was defined in the provision of "critical technical and management expertise, marketing channels and finance"—inputs that were perceived as being unavailable in Botswana. In return, investors were assured that they would "earn a fair return on their capital." For its part, the government undertook to ensure maximum long-term benefits for Botswana by exercising a supervisory role "through administration of exploration and development licenses, direct equity participation, and provision for the construction and operation of vital infrastructure."[24]

Therefore, although the government gave mining investors a free hand, it felt it could control the investment through a minority shareholding, administrative supervision of all prospecting and licensing, and the direct provision of infrastructure. The last method of control would ensure that the type, location, and quality of the infrastructure could provide for development and social needs beyond the needs of the mines themselves. The establishment of the Ministries of Mineral Resources and Water Affairs, Finance and Development Planning, and Works and

Communications reflected this desire. Concerning government revenue, the strategy was to establish royalty payments for various mineral groups and to negotiate enterprise-specific tax and shareholding agreements.

Development strategy in mining, as well as other sectors, also required policies in the area of labor relations. Wage policy in the early 1970s was inchoate. On the one hand, the large supply of unskilled labor could still be subjected to a less than livable wage in the private sector. In this regard, government policy was that "no employee . . . should be required to work for less than a minimum wage which enables him to clothe, feed and house himself and his immediate family sufficiently to maintain good health. In this respect minimum wages paid by Government in different areas for different work are intended as a guide to the private sector." On the other hand, senior salaries were to be subject to a freeze or reduction to overcome the historic inequality created by expatriates having held the senior positions. But there was also the fear that mining development might "give rise to a new group of unskilled employees in the modern sector of the economy with a standard of living substantially above that of the rural sector where the vast majority of the population must continue to seek their livelihood."[25]

In attempting to resolve the wage problem, the government asserted that its wage and salary levels would guide wages and salaries in the private sector. "Basic local wage and salary levels in the private and parastatal sectors should generally conform to, and on no account significantly exceed, those paid by Government to comparable grades of public employees, taking all factors into consideration." Second, unskilled workers should receive a minimum wage calculated as "the average rural income of farmers with an allowance for any differential in the overall cost of urban living," an average of about P 35 per annum in 1970. But, third, there was the determination "that there should be no statutory minimum wage covering all unskilled workers."[26]

These policies were administered through a National Employment, Manpower, and Incomes Council (NEMIC) and a series of sectoral wage councils created in 1973[27] on which government, employers, and workers were represented. In addition, the creation of worker and employer organizations was encouraged by the Department of Labour and the Ministry of Commerce and Industry. The strategy was to create organizations that the government could negotiate with and that would be parties to agreements concerning wages and conditions of work. The absence of agriculture as a target for a minimum wage was notable.

Thus, by the mid-1970s, a strategy had been developed for dealing with foreign investment in general and mining investment in particular. Its core was the distinction between the modern and nonmodern components—modern (mining) activity being identified as the means by which the rest of the economy would be modernized. As such, mining interests were treated very favorably with regard to the expectation of fair profits and the power to make decisions regarding the process of production. Government policy was aimed at maximizing the government's revenues through income and corporation taxes and royalties and ensuring a smooth initiation and maintenance of production. The policy included providing for a labor relations infrastructure and services, and the government expected to participate in the whole process through representation on the boards of mining enterprises.

In regard to wages, the most significant strategy concerned the establishment of minimum wages. Although a minimum wage was important for unskilled workers, it also had implications for wage rates for all skill levels. The most important element of the minimum wage for unskilled workers was the decision to base it on the average rural income of the traditional agricultural worker. Clearly, part of the motivation for this decision was to stop the drift toward the towns and to prevent urban-rural differentials from worsening, but the policy established the principle of very low minimum wages by accepting the view that what was an already inadequate rural income was an adequate urban wage. This decision created the basis for the continuation of the labor reserve economy, but now the laborers worked in Botswana as well as in South Africa.

The effect of this policy would depend in part on the strategy for rural development, for wages could rise as rural income increased. In any case, for the strategy of a mineral-led economy to be complete, it had to contain provisions for spending the revenues earned from mineral production.

In the late 1970s and early 1980s, the basic policies were carried forward. There were some revisions of royalty arrangements, taxation policies, incentives, and labor relations, but these were more in the nature of refinements than new strategic directions.[28]

Profits and Politics: The Transfer of Resources to Rural Development

The mineral-led strategy required a set of provisions for domestic development. The second principle of the "dual economic strategy" therefore entailed "re-investing the proceeds of these investments to promote labour intensive activities and improve services in rural areas." There were four primary goals in the rural development program. One was to generate sustained production through achieving "correct land use and management practices." Second, an improvement in rural marketing and credit facilities was desired. The third was the creation of employment in rural industries, services, and craft activities for those people with no other means of support, and fourth, the government was to improve the provision of social services in rural areas.[29]

The main problem was believed to be that there was a "dual economy." The bulk of the rural producers were thought to be carrying on traditional agricultural practices, which were probably non-market oriented, resistant to modern (market-oriented) techniques, and actually destructive of the natural environment when combined with commercial practices. Therefore, significant new forms of land tenure and management would have to be introduced, and this traditional economy would have

to change and become part of the modern economy of mining, manufacturing, and commercial agriculture.

The strategic political problem was how to make changes in the
communal ownership of land. It was felt that some form of exclusive
rights were required if productivity were to be improved and the
deterioration of the environment were to be stopped, but that same
exclusive use might have the effect of dispossessing large numbers of
people, a dangerous thing to do. In 1970, Seretse Khama asserted that
"we cannot permit the traditional methods to continue because under
the pressure of an expanding human and animal population, they are
ruining the land and the pasture which represents the only livelihood
for most of our people." Yet, at the same time, "we cannot afford to
permit individual tenure in tribal areas, since that would risk alienating
the majority from their means of production—the land." Such alienation
would thoroughly undermine political support for the BDP, so some
form of compromise would have to be reached in order to achieve the
goals of rural development.[30]

The process of policy formulation did not treat all elements of
rural development evenly. As that process unfolded, attention focused
on agriculture, specifically on cattle, and clearly, rural manufacturing
and food crop production each had a secondary priority. This emphasis
probably resulted from the near crisis atmosphere that had been created
concerning the condition of the grazing areas. The perception of a "very
rapid deterioration of the grazing areas," which threatened to undermine
"the basis for the main rural industry," called for "urgent and radical
action."[31]

Consultants in 1972 confirmed the deteriorating condition and
determined that at least two factors were involved.[32] One was the fact
that the communal ownership of land had created a situation in which
it was in no individual's interest to limit the number of cattle being
grazed but it was in everyone's interest to graze as many cattle as
possible. Given the unequal distribution of cattle ownership, this situation
had probably led to the unrestrained growth of large herds.

Second, during the late 1960s and early 1970s, a free-for-all had
taken place in connection with the securing of water rights. Both public
and private boreholes had been sunk, the only restriction being that
they had to be eight kilometers apart. In areas where there was no or
only seasonal surface water, access to borehole water had the effect of
yielding de facto rights to land, but without fencing, which was not
allowed on communal land except for small crop-growing areas, exclusive
water rights could not also mean exclusive rights to the land.

By the early 1970s, the water-right situation in rural areas was
nearly chaotic.[33] In 1972, allocations of individual borehole rights in the
Central District were being made at a rate that amounted to 14 to 17
percent of the total territory per year. More generally, "the disposal of
boreholes which were formerly public property to syndicates and individuals has in the past few years radically reduced the potential
availability of grazing land to other users. . . . the net effect has been

to provide cheaper water to fewer, better off people, while squeezing out some of those with smaller herds, forcing them to move to the already overgrazed areas near communal water supplies."[34]

The likelihood that any policy change would at least formalize such control over water and land accelerated the process. The people who had borehole rights "must realize the potential value of any step which further secures their position," and in addition, some owners of large herds began taking matters into their own hands either by surreptitiously fencing grazing land or by demanding the right to do so.[35]

Thus, the extension of water rights, their individualization, the expansion of the national herd, the intensification of grazing (particularly in the already hard-pressed communal areas), and the fact that the situation was so structured as to not provide any incentives to do anything about it all contributed to the perceived crisis in the early 1970s. The situation did not serve the longer-term interests of either the large cattleowners, who wished to become more fully commercial farmers, or the small-scale subsistence farmers, although the large farmers received disproportionate benefits from the situation.

Chambers and Feldman argued that the future lay in the direction of fully commercial farming and in a movement away "from patron-client towards employer-employee relationships," even though "some of the former clients will be displaced" in the process. They recommended that initially, there should be attempts to differentiate among four types of agricultural land use: reserved areas (for future use), commercial ranching areas, mixed farming areas, and communal grazing areas. Commercial and mixed areas should be subject to an exclusive lease and the payment of rent, and communal areas should allow for the minimal protection of the poor peasantariat. In addition, immediate measures were proposed to put a halt to the ongoing land rush and to stop the allocation of land through the allocation of water rights.[36]

The government accepted the main recommendations—specifically, "the Government accepts the introduction of fencing by individuals and groups. . . . Land which has been fenced will cease to be held on the basis of traditional tenure and will become the subject of a lease." Immediate measures were announced that essentially would prevent any further allocation of water rights, although they certainly did not roll back the allocations that had already been made.[37]

The program implementing these ideas was formulated as the National Policy on Tribal Grazing Land in July 1975. The basic provisions of the tribal grazing lands policy (TGLP) included encouragement for the land boards "to divide the Tribal grazing areas into three zones— Commercial Farming Areas, Communal Grazing Areas, and Reserved Areas." Existing de facto occupations of land by individuals and groups, with a few exceptions, would be more or less automatically classified as commercial, and in commercial areas, it was expected that inheritable leases would be signed, that leaseholders would have substantial herds, and that "where persons or groups wish to have more land than the Land Board allows, Government will take positive steps to enable them to secure holdings in freehold and state leasehold areas."[38] Inheritable, transferable, long-term (fifty-year) leases resolved the problem of land tenure for commercial farmers. On the one hand, such leases would "give security of tenure necessary for taking and granting of loans and for the introduction of improved management systems," and on the other hand, the leases would retain formal "ownership of land by the Tribal Land Boards."[39]

The provisions for the peasantariat were less promising. The amount of communal areas would remain at the present level, but land boards could restrict the number of livestock units (for example, cattle and goats) that could be kept by one person, family, or group. If a certain number were exceeded, the owners would be forced to move to a commercial area—*mafisa* (loaned) cattle would be counted as belonging to the holder. Rents from commercial areas would be used to improve grazing and management in communal areas. Finally, the reserved areas would be "set aside for the future. They are safeguards for the poorer members of the population."[40]

The TGLP promised something for everyone: As the TGLP document concluded, "everyone benefits. We can keep more cattle and have better cattle."[41] Other policies supporting the development of the cattle industry included modernizing and expanding the processing facilities at the Botswana Meat Commission, the possibility of a second slaughterhouse, an extension of markets, the retention of access to the European market, and further improvements in extension and other services to the people who raised cattle.

Development policy in the rural areas also concentrated on the provision of major social services, the three primary areas being education, health, and the domestic water supply. Adequate provisions in these areas were considered to be "the main way in which an immediate improvement in rural welfare can be effected." If nothing else, the expenditures involved would be a "major stimulus to the rural economy."[42]

Given the perception of a crisis in grazing areas and the prominence of the cattleowners, it is not surprising that agricultural activities other than the cattle business received considerably less attention until the late 1970s. Thus, although the plan noted that "more people are directly engaged in arable agriculture" than in livestock production, and although arable production was more important as an element for subsistence, it was given little attention. Indeed, in the 1976–1981 plan, 73 percent of the capital allocation for agriculture was budgeted for livestock development.[43] The only real initiative in the area of arable agriculture was the creation of the Botswana Agricultural Marketing Board in 1974.

The relative neglect of arable production had important consequences that had to be faced in policy formulation. One was the fact that the livestock and arable production enterprises are closely related. The possible loss of oxen to the commercial areas could affect the farmers' ability to plow, which was already at a low level for many. But more seriously, the neglect of arable lands allowed people to begin to accumulate land, much as others had done earlier in the grazing areas. By 1978, one concerned officer noted that "there is an incipient *land grab* which will get worse if arable agriculture becomes more profitable."[44]

A new interest in the problems of arable production was also stimulated by two other developments. One was a decline in the rate at which South Africa recruited workers in Botswana, which began shutting the door to that outlet for the unemployed and underemployed workers in the rural areas. Second, it was clear that agricultural employment opportunities, whether for wages or self-employment, were simply not being created by the existing strategy at anything like the rate required. A thorough study of this problem concluded that in 1978, "Botswana provided work for at most 208,000 people. However, about 376,000 people were available for work. To fill the gap of 166,000 [*sic*] Botswana needs 16–17,000 sufficiently attractive working opportunities— either as jobs or as self-employment every year for the next ten years."[45] Taking into account natural increases (12,000 to 13,000 workers per year), returning migrants (4,000 to 5,000 per year), and reductions in cattle production employment (1,000 per year), the total shortfall was about 350,000, or 35,000 jobs per year—an additional number that was equivalent to more than two and one-half times the number existing in 1978.

Such figures highlighted the problem of development and indicated the limits of the TGLP as a solution, but they also underlined the development strategy's preoccupation with minerals and cattle. This focus meant that only a limited priority had been set, for example, on developing manufacturing in rural and urban areas.

In 1978, the employment adviser recommended the development of a new strategy that would be oriented around the creation of a self-sufficient peasantry whose income would be sufficient to eliminate the "pull" of high urban wages. The recommendations included restrictions on working-class wages combined with a redirection of resources away from road building and toward increasing the efficiency and amount of production. They also included a revised set of investment incentives, including state subsidies for the employment of unskilled workers, and a relaxation or an elimination of much of the industrial and commercial licensing and many of the regulatory requirements. For agriculture, the adviser advocated concentrating on small farms (fifteen hectares or less) and transferring draft animals (oxen and donkeys) from large cattleowners to small holders and the people who owned no cattle.[46]

The 1979–1985 plan accepted the need to reorient the development strategy toward creating a broad range of employment opportunities.[47] This change entailed a commitment toward decreasing allocations to infrastructural development and increasing allocations to productive assets. It also included increasing the priority given to manufacturing and commercial opportunities, particularly in the rural areas. It did not include a decreased emphasis on developing more capital-intensive undertakings in livestock development, although it included new initiatives in an arable lands development policy. It did not, therefore, remove the underlying bias toward the large-scale cattleowners or arable farmer, so the new development strategy did not accept the adviser's linchpin recommendation concerning the redistribution of the critical means of production (cattle) to the people who lacked that asset.

RATIONALE OF DEVELOPMENT IN PERSPECTIVE

At least two broad concluding perspectives about Botswana's development strategy may be indicated. One is that the process of policy formulation was disjointed. It was a learning process, and it can be divided into roughly three periods. The early period (1966–1970) lacked coherence and direction because of uncertainties concerning the availability of resources and data as well as political uncertainties that centered on a number of new government institutions and the coalition that controlled them. The result was a rather incomplete formulation both in principle and in specifics.

With the discovery of mineral deposits and a stabilized environment, a more coherent plan was produced for the period from about 1970 to 1978. This plan introduced the strategy of the extractive mining industry's generating the resources for domestic development, which involved committing resources to develop the mines, reaching agreement with foreign investors, and establishing infrastructure and policies to facilitate the creation of a mineral-led economy. The second "leg" of the plan involved a strategy for developing the cattle industry, in particular through the formulation of the TGLP. Thus, the process of constructing and legitimizing a rationale for development began.

But certain strains and new situations emerged about 1978 that made it necessary to refine the development strategy. Primarily, attempts were made to overcome the problems created by a relative neglect of arable agriculture and manufacturing, and it was recognized that the national development strategy had been inadequate in relation to the problem of creating conditions for long-term productive employment.

Second, establishing a development strategy in the whole postcolonial period was a political process—even the underdevelopment of Botswana at independence was the result of political decisions made since the nineteenth century. The natural environment provided a backdrop of opportunities and constraints, but decisions made within that context were not dictated by the environment as such. The role of foreign investment was determined partially by technical and economic factors, but it was basically a political decision that determined the role of government in mining. In agriculture, overgrazing had some ecological aspects, but it was the social and political relations of production that created the problem and became central to the solution.

Thus, the evolution of a development strategy was a political process that involved the political elite of medium- and large-scale cattleowners in combination with a bureaucratic and commercial elite. The decisions they made were made with the likely response of the broad mass of the population in mind, but the outcome was clearly more in their interests than in the interests of the peasantariat. An evaluation of the resulting development strategy can be made by examining the actual allocations and the consequences of the whole implementation process.

5

Development Strategy:
Implementation
and Consequences

The process of formulating a development strategy was a political one and it was defined primarily by internal and external socioeconomic and political relationships. The process of implementation, the generation and allocation of resources, was also political; it was defined by the sources of investable surpluses and was carried out with the social consequences of the investments in mind.

The effects and consequences of resource allocation are also cumulative. Capital investments today lead to recurrent expenses tomorrow. Building a road to Kanye out of the development fund means a yearly item in the maintenance budget of the Ministry of Works and Communications. Such one-time and recurrent costs quickly place constraints on future planning, a fact that is most observable in public sector infrastructural projects. But investment in the productive sectors, whether public or private, also represents a continuing commitment. Most important, there are one-time and recurrent social and political "costs" as development expenditures affect different individuals and groups differently. Today's development expenditure and tomorrow's continuing commitment create opportunities and limits in social terms. The distribution of resources ultimately provokes and forestalls political action; at the same time, it advances and retards social cohesion and dissonance.

In Botswana, the postcolonial period has been characterized by tremendous growth-creating processes of class formation and developing political relationships. A close government–foreign investor partnership in mining has generated significant resources, and in addition, external aid has been introduced on a large scale. These resources have formed the bulk of the funds allocated to domestic development. These allocations, combined with policies concerning wages, unions, agriculture, public services, and manufacturing, have had consequences for the different classes and for politics. The peasantariat has become more of a working

72

class, and the elite has developed further, but various elements of the elite are pursuing increasingly specific projects. The relationship between the peasantariat and the elite has increasingly showed signs of both continuity and strain as a result of development.

This chapter explores these patterns in the context of the generation and allocation of resources. First, an administrative capacity was created to formulate development plans, negotiate with donors and investors, and supervise expenditures, and agreements were reached with multinational mining concerns. Second, specific project and policy expenditures for domestic development were undertaken. Third, these processes and actions have reflected the cooperation and conflict between and within classes, and it is these interactions that have provided the broad parameters of the political economy of change in the postcolonial period.

ADMINISTRATIVE CAPACITY AND RESOURCE GENERATION

The creation of an administrative planning and implementation authority began before independence, and a small economic planning unit in the Ministry of Finance became the Ministry of Development Planning shortly after independence. The need to closely relate the functions of planning and finance, and the need to manage the conflicts between the two areas, led to the creation of a combined Ministry of Finance and Development Planning (MFDP) in 1971. The vice-president also became the minister of what "emerged as a formidable power within government."[1] Staffed initially largely by expatriates, the economic affairs planning division negotiated external finance arrangements and controlled internal planning. It created a "relaxed and extremely pragmatic" relationship with donors, particularly Britain. From a donor perspective, the ability of the MFDP to produce and carry through plans was impressive: "Where Botswana really scored was in administration and planning."[2]

Within the Botswana government, in law and as a matter of policy, the MFDP became one of the two "senior" ministries, the other being the Office of the President. The planning functions of sectoral ministries were subject to MFDP approval, which coordinated the generation of finance and expenditures. By the early 1970s, the MFDP was the hub of a tightly organized and powerful planning and implementing administrative structure. There is little doubt that the other ministries and departments paid serious attention to MFDP processes and directives. The MFDP did not win all the battles, but it could not be ignored or easily bypassed.

The obtaining of external resources was and is perceived as critical. Although the 1979–1985 Development Plan predicted that 85 percent of total expenditure and public investment finance would be covered by internal revenue, the great bulk of development finance since 1966 has come from external sources (see Table 5.1).

TABLE 5.1
Proportion of Development Expenditures Financed from
External Sources 1966/1967 - 1980/1981

Year	Total Development Expenditure (million P)[a]	Externally Funded (percent)[b]
1966/67 - 1969/70	15.9	100
1970/1971	8.5	88
1971/1972	12.3	98
1972/1973	29.8	99
1973/1974	30.2	91
1974/1975	32.7	62
1975/1976	33.0	58
1976/1977	45.0	82
1977/1978	53.0	77
1978/1979	55.0	75
1979/1980	60.0	50
1980/1981	62.0	60

[a] includes Category A and Category B Projects in the plans.
[b] includes finance listed as external bond issue (2.0 million in 1970/1971 only); other sources, mainly foreign; donor funds, approved or under negotiation; and funds to be negotiated.

Source: Botswana, National Development Plan 1976-81 (Gaborone: Government Printer, 1977), Table 1.6, p. 12, and Table 2.10, p. 48.

During the eight years to 1974/1975, external sources accounted for a yearly average of 97 percent of expenditures, which does not include the large private foreign investments in mining, but as more internal resources became available, a smaller proportion of the expenditures had to be financed externally. In the years 1974/1975 through 1978/1979, external funding, on the average, accounted for about 71 percent of expenditures. The 1979/1985 development expenditures were projected to be P 529.7 million, a significant proportion of which would have to be funded externally.[3]

Although this long-term, continuing dependence on external sources is noteworthy, considerable internal resources have been and are being generated. Most important, these internal resources allow greater flexibility in the social and political purposes to which such funds are committed.

IMPLEMENTING DEVELOPMENT STRATEGY: RESOURCES AND THEIR INVESTMENT

The description of implementation as resource allocation and investment can be divided into three parts, which roughly parallel the evolution of the development strategy. These three parts are expenditures creating the mineral-led economy, other foreign investments subsidiary to mining, and expenditures related primarily to other domestic sectors.

The Mineral-Led Economy

The first decade of development expenditures was dominated by the development of a mining capacity and an infrastructure. Between 1966 and 1973, 45 percent of all development expenditures were accounted for by the Shashe Project (primarily in connection with the copper/nickel mine at Selebi-Phikwe), and in 1971–1973, this proportion averaged 75 percent. Although the amount declined after 1973, the Shashe Project still accounted for one-third of all expenditures through 1975. In contrast, during the 1966–1973 period, expenditures on agriculture, commerce, industry, and water combined accounted for about 13 percent of the total. Nearly 75 percent of the 1973–1975 budgets were accounted for by the Shashe Project and the Ministry of Works.[4]

The origins of the Shashe Project are to be found in a 1959 prospecting and mining concession given by the Bangwato tribe to the Rhodesian Selection Trust Exploration Company. After independence, the tribal territories and freehold landowners were persuaded to transfer their mineral rights to the central government, which then planned the pattern of exploration and mining.

The discovery of commercially payable copper/nickel ore deposits led to a complicated agreement between the government and mining companies. The interlocking agreement involved the government of Botswana, the World Bank, and U.S., Canadian, German, and South African aid organizations, banks, or corporations.[5]

The copper/nickel mine at Selebi-Phikwe is operated by Bamangwato Concessions Limited (BCL), 15 percent of which is owned by the Botswana government and 85 percent by the Botswana Roan Selection Trust (BRST). The ownership of the BRST is divided thus: 40 percent by public shareholding and 30 percent each by American Metal Climax (AMAX) and the Anglo American Corporation/Charter Consolidated Group (London) (AAC). Direct investment in the mine came from a P 52-million loan from German banks, a South African Industrial Development Corporation loan of P 13.5 million (for purchases in South Africa), and money from the shareholders of the BRST, mainly the major partners, AMAX and AAC.

The Botswana government retained responsibility for providing the necessary infrastructure, partially to create investor confidence but also so that the government could create an infrastructure that would be of benefit beyond the narrow purpose of copper/nickel mining. That infrastructure included the provision of electricity and water, as well as the building of roads and a new town. The money for the government's contribution was raised through the International Development Agency ($2.5 million), the World Bank ($32 million), the U.S. Agency for International Development ($6.6 million), and the Canadian International Development Agency (a $30 million loan for the purchase of electrical-generating equipment in Canada). The AAC also opened a small and highly capital-intensive coal mine at Marupule to supply energy for the smelter.

The government's risk was minimal. The mining companies guaranteed that they would purchase sufficient power and water to cover the costs of the loans, and failing that, the main partners would make direct repayment to the World Bank. Government revenue was to be received according to a formula that included 7.5 percent of the gross profits, 40 percent of the residual gross profits as corporation income tax (fixed by law for twenty-five years), and dividends from the government's 15 percent equity in BCL—through shares issued gratis to the government.[6]

The Selebi-Phikwe mine was not a success. Technical problems, managerial lapses, and a weak price for copper combined to increase the capital cost of the mine to P 273 million, about P 100 million more than had been expected.[7] Its operations had led to an accumulated loss of P 102,497,000 by 31 December 1977, a loss that was equivalent to more than twice the Botswana government's recurrent budget of P 46.6 million in 1974/1975. The debt situation combined with the low prices led to the conclusion that "no dividends will be paid by the company in the foreseeable future."[8]

The accumulating losses and increasing debt have led to periodic financial restructuring. In 1977, among other things, the agreement on royalties was altered so the government would receive 3 percent of the gross value of copper, nickel, and cobalt in the matte (the semiprocessed form, which is marketed from Botswana), which would give the government an income even if there were no profits. In addition, P 75 million in loans from AMAX and AAC to the BCL were converted into 10 percent cumulative preference shares, which left a loan indebtedness of P 50 million. A further renegotiation took place in 1982 when $102.8 million of the senior debt was converted to a subordinate debt.[9]

The mine continues to operate, although its losses are stunning, for a variety of reasons. It provides direct employment for a large number of people—the 1983 estimate was 4,600—and the loss of these and related jobs would be a severe blow to formal sector employment and the local economy at Selebi-Phikwe. In addition, although the level of export earnings has been consistently below what was estimated, the export sales value of the matte is considerable—P 47 million in 1978/ 1979.[10] Furthermore, much of the operating loss results from the heavy interest payments for borrowed money. For example, of BRST's total loss in 1977, 72 percent was accounted for by interest and other charges for borrowed money. Most of this money accrues to AMAX and AAC, whose losses are primarily in the "sunk" capital, which could not be realized if the mine closed. Finally, there is the matter of the guaranteed loans that the government might have to default on if the mine closed, which would mean that the primary shareholders would have to repay the loans. If the mine continues to operate, there are at least some revenues that can help repay the loans.

Had the mineral-led strategy relied on the BCL alone for its strength, development in Botswana would have been a disaster. Fortunately for Botswana, a twelve-year period of exploration resulted in the discovery of a kimberlite pipe at Orapa in 1967, and other pipes were discovered nearby. The result was the opening of the Orapa mine in 1971 and another at Letlhakane in 1977, and "revenues from the two mines in 1980 were in excess of P 200 million, with Government receiving not less than 65% to 70%."[11]

Further prospecting revealed the existence of additional diamond deposits in southeastern Botswana at or near Jwaneng. The Jwaneng diamond mine was coming on-stream in 1982 with a projected output of four million carats per year by the mid-1980s. The potential for the Jwaneng and associated pipes is very large indeed. The chairman of De Beers Consolidated Mines Limited, Harry F. Oppenheimer, has gone so far as to say that "Jwaneng is probably the most important kimberlite pipe discovered anywhere in the world since the original discoveries at Kimberley more than a century ago."[12]

Diamond mining in Botswana is critically important to both De Beers and Botswana. The country's mines are new and efficient and more profitable than most. From 1974 through 1978, Orapa and Letlhakane ranked first or second out of ten or eleven mines in Botswana, South Africa, and Namibia in carats recovered and carats per 100 metric tons of ore. Orapa went from ninth out of twelve mines in lowest cost per metric ton milled to first place in 1977.[13] In addition, Botswana's output is becoming the biggest single factor in De Beers's output. Had Jwaneng been producing 4 million carats in 1981, Botswana's production would have represented 46.1 percent of the total output of diamonds by the De Beers group.[14] Finally, De Beers has to be concerned about the volume of diamonds from Botswana if the company is to retain its primary role in the marketing of diamonds through the Central Selling Organization, which it controls.

Botswana's benefits have included direct employment for 7,200 people in 1980,[15] plus tertiary employment, and the Jwaneng mine will result in additional employment. In addition, the contribution of all mining to the real GDP increased from 6.5 percent in 1974/1975 to 34 percent in 1979/1980. Most important, the direct contribution of mining to government revenues increased from P 14 million (or 13.1 percent) in 1974/1975 to P 47.7 million (or 28.9 percent of total revenue) in 1979/1980. This contribution does not include the indirect revenues, in the forms of customs revenue on capital and current inputs in mining, which were substantial. Had those revenues been included, the contri-

Mining the kimberlite pipe
at Jwaneng.

bution to the total revenue would have been "considerably larger,"
perhaps on the order of 40 percent or more.[16]

That this level of revenue would be forthcoming from diamonds
was not a foregone conclusion in the late 1960s. At that time, the
considerable reserves at Jwaneng were unknown, and in addition, the
Botswana government needed mining investment so badly that it initially
accepted a very unfavorable arrangement concerning ownership and
profits—the original agreement gave the government a shareholding of
15 percent. The capital for the mine was provided by De Beers, and
the company designed the mine, for security reasons, as a closed
compound community, a company town. De Beers also had more or
less exclusive control over the whole mining process.

The success of the mine at Orapa led to a renegotiation of the
agreement in 1975. The government insisted on a 50-50 split in shareholding and a favorable profit/tax arrangement. Although the negotiations
were not entirely congenial, they did result in such an agreement. De

The main treatment plant at the Jwaneng diamond mine in southeastern Botswana.

Beers Botswana Mining Company (Debswana) now is owned half by De Beers and half by the government of Botswana, and this company operates all the diamond mines in the country. Most of the capital and technical expertise are provided by De Beers, although the government took up its option of providing a 20 percent equity shareholding in the Jwaneng mine. In addition, in the case of Jwaneng, the government insisted on an "open" township, not a closed compound. Although the town and service facilities were built and are operated by De Beers, most of them will be handed over to the government over a period of time.[17]

Other Foreign Investment

Although investment in mining was by far the most important element in the export mineral-led strategy, other private foreign investments were encouraged as a means of increasing the material base of the economy. This strategy, facilitated by the Botswana Development Corporation, has borne some fruit, although production is limited by the nature of the internal market; shortages of raw materials, local finance, and managerial and technical personnel; and the country's proximity to South Africa and its membership in the customs area.

By 1975, there were sixty-five manufacturing units, all but three of which were in urban areas and 69 percent of which were foreign owned. By 1979, there were a total of eighty-eight enterprises, eighty-four of which were in urban areas, and 65 percent of which were foreign owned. Twenty-three others were of mixed foreign and Batswana ownership, which meant that 91 percent of the manufacturing units were completely or partly foreign owned.[18]

Although not insignificant, the manufacturing sector tends to be made up of small units and to concentrate on "light" import-substituting packaging and final-stage-assembly operations. In 1978/1979, manufacturing employed 5,088 people, nearly one-third of whom worked at the Botswana Meat Commission (BMC). Other concentrations were found in nineteen metal products enterprises, employing 704 people; in thirteen garment and textile firms, employing 686 people; and in eight building-materials concerns, employing 358 people. These enterprises and the BMC accounted for 47 percent of all manufacturing concerns and 67 percent of all manufacturing employees.[19] In 1980, manufacturing accounted for 6.7 percent of the total formal sector employment and 4.5 percent of the GDP.[20]

The manufacturing sector is also polarized between a large number of small units and a few large ones. Throughout the 1970s, more than three-quarters of all manufacturing enterprises had 50 or fewer employees; only a very few, never more than 6 percent, had 201 or more. Such a steady pattern over the whole decade is indicative of the problems Botswana has experienced in attempting to create a large manufacturing sector. With the exception of a very few operations, like the Kgalagadi Brewery, the constraints on developing manufacturing enterprises, whether foreign or locally owned, have been significant.[21]

There has been foreign investment in Botswana's economy in areas other than mining, then, but its impact up to 1983 was not very significant. Some jobs and a wider tax base have been created, but such investments have not been a driving force in economic growth and have not laid the basis for a self-sustaining process of economic growth.

Domestic Development Expenditure

The renegotiation of the Southern African Customs Union Agreement, the success of the diamond mines, export sales of beef, and large foreign loans and grants generated significant resources for allocation beyond what was needed to create a mineral-led economy. There have therefore been significant expenditures on development projects in the domestic sector: A rough estimate of their magnitude is on the order of P 1,407.4 million from 1966 to 1985.[22]

Throughout the independence period, but particularly in the first fifteen years, domestic development expenditures concentrated on infrastructural development. The creation of physical (water, roads, and communications), social (education and health), and administrative (government facilities and housing for civil servants) infrastructures absorbed the bulk of available resources. In the period 1968–1973, excluding the Shashe Project, more than half (57.8 percent) of the expenditures were made by the Ministry of Works and Communications. An additional 6.5 percent was spent by the Ministry of Local Government and Lands, mostly on housing, and the Ministries of Health, Education, Labour, and Home Affairs combined accounted for 10.8 percent of domestic development expenditures.[23]

Tables 5.2 and 5.3 give an indication of domestic development expenditures, actual and projected, from 1973 to 1985.[24] From 1973 to 1975, over three-quarters of the expenditures were for social and economic infrastructure, and more than two-thirds was allocated to transportation, urban, and educational infrastructure. This pattern was repeated in the period 1976–1981, when 58 percent was allocated to those three areas, and all infrastructural projects absorbed about three-quarters of the P 300.8 million development budget.

Three observations may be made about the pattern of allocations up to 1981. First, the bias toward infrastructural development was not spread evenly over the country as it focused on the development of the major urban areas and their linkage by roads and means of mass communications. Relatively speaking, rural areas were left behind except perhaps in the areas of water supplies for the major villages and the building of primary schools. Second, Table 5.2 highlights the fact that only limited resources were allocated to directly productive activities, particularly in agriculture, which received 5.3 percent of the allocations in 1973–1975 and 4 percent in 1976–1981. Third, the government had sufficient funds by 1976 to meet the heavy infrastructural demands as well as to be able to begin the process of channeling resources, however tentatively, to specific sectors of the economy. In 1976–1981, 6.2 percent of the expenditures went for projects that were related to the tribal grazing lands policy, an additional 2.6 percent went for rural development, and 1.1 percent was allocated to manufacturing, industrial, and commercial projects and services. The projects in the last category were planned to stimulate Batswana entrepreneurial activity.

This pattern of allocations continued in the 1979–1985 period with three noteworthy modifications: greatly expanded resources, a change in the pattern of allocations for infrastructural development, and a decreased emphasis on infrastructure. Concerning the first, Botswana's increased ability to generate external aid combined with the country's increased diamond and customs revenues led to a dramatic increase in available resources. Even taking into account the rather sharp inflation over the years, it is worth noting that projected expenditures for 1979–1985 were more than triple those of the previous plan period (1976–1981). Indeed, in current prices, 68.9 percent of all development expenditures from 1966 to 1985 were scheduled to be made in the years 1979–1985. Therefore, although, proportionately, infrastructural development was to receive less, in absolute terms, very large financial resources are still being allocated to infrastructure.

Second, infrastructural development began to be characterized in part by a few "big ticket" items. The takeover of the railway, the building of a new airport, and the development of the army received a total of 22.3 percent of the overall development budget, the railway alone accounting for just over 10 percent.

TABLE 5.2
Domestic Development Expenditure 1973–1975 and 1976–1981
by Major Category

Category of Expenditure	Years and Proportion	
	1973–1975 (% of total)	1976–1981 (% of total)
Main roads development	27.7	24.2
Urban development	26.6	23.4
Primary and secondary schools	12.5	11.1
Health	3.2	2.1
Major and rural village water supply	5.7	2.7
Agriculture	5.3	4.0
Tribal grazing lands policy related		6.2
Rural roads	2.1	
Rural development		2.6
Administrative infrastructure		12.3

Batswana enterprise development, industrial building leasing, trader extension	16.9	1.1
Other		10.3
Total expenditure[a]	100.0	100.0
	P 42,099,000	P 300,803,000

a Total expenditure excludes the Shashe Project in 1973-1975 and includes the total estimated cost of Category A projects in the plan in 1976-1981. These projects were "either on-going or those for which finance has been negotiated already or under negotiation or for which a donor has been identified" (Botswana, National Development Plan 1976-81, p. 259).

Sources: Botswana, Estimates of Recurrent Expenditure and Estimate of Revenue and Expenditure of the Development Fund of the Year 1976/77 (Gaborone: Government Printer, n.d.), pp. 159-215, and Botswana, National Development Plan 1976-81 (Gaborone: Government Printer, 1977), pp. 365-366 and 369-384.

TABLE 5.3
Domestic Development Expenditure 1979-1985 by Major
Category[a]

Category	Percent of Total Expenditure
Administrative infrastructure	11.9
Mainline railway takeover	10.6
Primary and secondary schools	9.6
Main and secondary roads	8.7
Urban development	8.3
Botswana Defence Force	7.5
Cattle related	4.4
Rural development	4.4
New Gaborone airport	4.2
Jwaneng equity	3.5
Northern abattoir	2.3
Other agriculture	2.3
Major village development	1.9
Arable lands development	1.9
Health	1.5
Industry/manufacturing/commerce	1.3
Other	15.7
Total expenditure	100.0
	P 970,411,000

[a] There is some overlap with the 1976-1981 plan totals,
but in the plans, it is not feasible to separate the years.
Although this overlap artificially inflates the pula value
of expenditure, it does not distort the proportionate
allocation to different sectors in the plans. The 1979-1985
money values are in current prices; expenditures are for
Category A projects only.

Source: Botswana, National Development Plan 1979-85
(Gaborone: Government Printer, 1980), pp. 407-426.

Third, in the 1979-1985 period, infrastructural allocations, although still absorbing about two-thirds of the total expenditures, showed signs of being reduced in favor of more directly productive expenditures or of stimulating productive activities. Of the expenditures planned, 5.8 percent was allocated to equity in the Jwaneng mine and the building of a northern abattoir (slaughterhouse); arable agriculture and cattle development accounted for 6.3 percent of the total; other agricultural and rural development, for an additional 6.7 percent, and 1.3 percent was for industry, manufacturing, and commerce. These categories combined accounted for 20.1 percent of the total.

Traditional housing in Serowe with new thatch being readied in the right background.

Yet, overall, one cannot escape the conclusion that the 1979–1985 plan still repeats the pattern of heavy infrastructural expenditures. The development of roads, urban areas, transportation facilities, schools, and government administration still absorb the lion's share of the available finance. Although the beginning of a trickle of resources has begun for other projects, the allocation of substantial resources to infrastructure, including administrative capacity, is a relatively permanent feature of expenditures in Botswana.

Old and new intermingle in a house in Molepolole, a large village near Gaborone.

The railway station and bus park in Gaborone with the Debswana Building in the background.

IMPLEMENTING DEVELOPMENT STRATEGY: THE POLITICAL ECONOMY OF GROWTH

A description of expenditures is only one part of any analysis of change in the independence period. These allocations effect the distribution of income and opportunities, which results in recurrent and new demands on resources. An analysis must therefore include a discussion of the socioeconomic and political consequences of the allocations.

The Recurrent Budget

The most obvious consequences of capital expenditures is that they often represent a permanent charge on future resources. Roads, boreholes, and buildings must be maintained; teachers, civil servants, and workers have to be paid. Today's development expenditure is tomorrow's line item in a ministerial budget.

Although a complete assessment of the growth of recurrent expenditures resulting from development projects is not feasible, certain features may be noted. During the three-year period 1976/1977 through 1978/1979, for example, recurrent expenditures in current prices amounted to P 225.6 million.[25] The recurrent costs associated with development projects implemented in those three years alone amounted to P 21.8 million, or 9.7 percent of all recurrent expenditures. Even so, the immediate recurrent expenses of many projects, like roads, do not reflect the long-term expense implications. The projected recurrent expenditure implication of the 1979–1985 Development Plan during the period of its implementation was P 175.6 million, which represents about 14 percent of the total recurrent budget from 1979/1980 to 1984/1985.[26]

This expansion of the recurrent budget has several effects. One is that the absorption of revenue by recurrent expenditures leaves that much less to be allocated to the development budget. Second, the administrative maintenance of infrastructure expands public employment very rapidly, but it does not produce the resources needed to maintain it. Third, over a period of time, the combination of development and recurrent expenditures sets a pattern that becomes increasingly difficult to break. People have vested interests in the perpetuation of the pattern, and therefore there are sociopolitical supports for its continuation and expansion on the part of those people to whom the development expenditures were first directed and who derive its recurrent benefits. This situation may "lock" future plans into an incrementalist net—future expenditures being determined by gradual change in existing patterns—which would suppress any critical evaluation of the plans and close off consideration of alternative structural possibilities.

Such effects may be muted as long as recurrent revenues increase at least as fast as the recurrent expenditures, and they may not be serious if recurrent revenues increase faster. Botswana's performance in this area is instructive. Up to 1972, domestic recurrent revenues were inadequate to cover domestic recurrent, let alone development, expenditures. Since that year, however, domestic recurrent revenues have been more than enough to meet recurrent needs despite the dramatic growth in recurrent expenditures. From 1972/1973 through 1978/1979, for example, domestic recurrent revenues amounted to P 518.7 million, and recurrent expenditures totaled P 354.5 million. Although it was estimated that there would be a closer relationship in the 1979–1985 period, it was likely that recurrent revenues would still more than cover recurrent expenditures.[27]

However, two trends must be noted. One is that the recurrent surplus has never been adequate to finance all expenditures including development projects, and hence, there has to be concern about committing resources to the recurrent budget. Second, given the more or less fixed commitments in the recurrent budget, a downturn in recurrent revenues could quickly lead to deficits, or at least the effects previously noted, which would place limits on future expansion.

This problem seemed to be arising in the early 1980s. Mineral revenues were not meeting expectations, and after a long period of hefty balances, the consolidated fund began dwindling—between 1980 and 1982, the balance was reduced by P 66.6 million, which drew it down to only P 2.8 million.[28] Although this decline was not disastrous, it undoubtedly directs attention to the buildup and performance of the recurrent expenditures since independence.

The Political Economy of Growth

The political economy of growth is the cumulative interaction of the socioeconomic political consequences of the development strategy and the allocation of resources. Such consequences ultimately define the trajectory of both growth and change, viewed historically and into the future.

The cumulative nature of these consequences is best illustrated by a sequential description as three periods are evident. One, from 1966 to 1974, was a period of rather high expectations and movement toward creating an effective political, administrative, and economic infrastructure. Second, from 1975 to 1980, the infrastructure was consolidated, but additionally, some of the strains caused by the earlier implementation had to be managed and their consequences faced. Some people also began to argue for more group- or class-specific programs. Third, from 1980 to at least 1983, the accumulated costs of the earlier periods created a new permanent environment and a more complex socioeconomic and political equation.

Toward a Baseline for Change: 1966–1974. The gross underdevelopment of the colonial period was the cause of a relatively high degree of class unity, and relatively high, but absolutely modest, expectations in the early postcolonial period. The middle class was very small in number, unclear as to its goals, and close to its mass base, the peasantariat. Lacking a clear class program, the ideology of the middle class appeared to be in everyone's interest, and the promise of a socially even process of development seemed viable. Only the development of an effective national government vis-à-vis the traditional political authorities promised sustained political conflict, a few long-standing political enmities notwithstanding.

For the peasantariat, independence promised the possibility of improved agricultural arrangements and more social services in the forms of schools, health clinics, and reliable water supplies. In addition, there was the expectation of a widening of opportunities for wage work in Botswana.

The mineral-led strategy and creation of a large administrative state infrastructure would have seemed unexceptionable to the peasantariat. Mineral development did not require drastic population movement or the alienation of large areas of agricultural land. The minerals were not being used for anything—and in that sense, they were valueless to the vast majority—so the fact that their extraction could make the provision of schools, etc., possible must have seemed a great bonanza, and it would have seemed normal that an increase in the number of administrative institutions was necessary. Thus, the idea that the state should undergo a transformation was not a particularly threatening idea. Indeed, it is unlikely that these matters were either clearly understood or consistently evaluated.

Finally, even the drastic increase in revenue because of the customs union was achieved without raising the existing rates of taxation since the increase merely represented a redistribution of the existing revenue pool and the increased revenue from the importation of mining inputs. The escalation of revenues from mining and beef exports also occurred without any involvement on the part of the peasantariat.

But the results of the changes were noticeable. Roads, schools, and water-supply systems were built—most dramatically as a result of the Accelerated Rural Development Programme of 1974—jobs were created, and wages rose. Excluding agriculture, in 1967/1968, there were an estimated 28,148 formally employed wage earners. This figure increased to 36,475 in 1972 and to 53,075 in 1975, an increase of nearly 100 percent from 1967/1968.[29] Wages also rose for those people who had jobs in Botswana. The minimum wage for the industrial (manual labor) class in the public sector rose dramatically from P 0.63 per day to P 2.00 per day between 1966 and 1974.[30] Furthermore, the wages of the migrant workers in the mines in South Africa increased very rapidly as well because of the rise in the world price for gold in the 1970s.

Despite this increase in opportunities for work in urban areas and the provision of some services in rural areas, the underlying structure of the peasantariat remained untouched. Little was done to improve the productive capacity of this class in agriculture, and urban wages remained low. A thorough survey in 1974/1975 concluded that 45 percent of the rural households had an income that provided a standard of living that was below an arbitrary but very harsh poverty line. Income inequality was also evident as the poorest 50 percent of the population shared 17.4 percent of the total income, the richest 10 percent shared 42 percent, and the richest 5 percent shared 29.9 percent.[31]

The low level of rural income was partly a reflection of the ownership and control of cattle and the low level of the wages that provided a considerable proportion of the rural income. A large number, 83.8 percent, of the households owned twenty-five or fewer cattle; 45 percent owned no cattle at all.[32] Not having ownership or control of oxen resulted in the inability to plow on time or at all, and one study showed that as a result, 91 percent of the households "infrequently or never" produced enough food for self-sufficiency.[33]

Therefore, for the 50 percent of the households that were lowest in the distribution of income, only about 15 percent of their total income was derived from crops or livestock, nearly two-thirds was received "in kind," and nearly 20 percent resulted from "transfers" or wages. The richest households, those that owned cattle, derived nearly two-thirds of their income from livestock and a further 20 percent from trade, which was presumably financed by prior sales of livestock.[34]

Similar inequalities existed in urban areas. In 1976, the total number of Botswana wage earners was 46,905, of whom 31,252, or 67 percent, were below the poverty line of P 108.85 per month for a household of five people.[35] Such an income distribution reflects relatively low wages for the vast majority of the urban workers, who were earning close to the unskilled minimum wage. The much smaller number of wage earners in the salariat[36] had a minimum wage of P 11.13 per day in 1974, more than five times that for unskilled workers, and the opportunities of the former were considerably greater than those of the industrial workers.[37]

There continued to be an unequal distribution of services as well. For example, the tremendous amounts spent on education expanded the availability of primary schools in rural areas, but the quality of those schools was low. Although only 7.2 percent of the teachers in urban schools was untrained, the figure was 49 percent in small villages. Pupil-teacher ratios also favored urban areas. The proportion of students receiving As and Bs was 42 percent in urban areas but 26 percent in large and small villages.[38] In addition, the students attending the English-medium and private schools (schools in which English was the sole medium of instruction and that had greater resources than the Setswana-medium schools had) were largely children of expatriates or of a small elite of Batswana, including wealthy cattleowners, civil servants, and politicians.

During this period, members of the small middle class, or petty bourgeoisie, which included the Botswana Democratic party governing coalition, were concerned about the survival of their class and the creation of a baseline for its development. Although somewhat divided among themselves, there were enough people who bridged the differences to reduce any open conflict. All factions wanted an infrastructural base, and there was no division over the desirability of a mineral-led strategy in which government would play a leading role. There was no indigenous capital that could be used to invest in and run the mine, nor any cadre of technically qualified people who could appropriate the mine for themselves. Thus, there was a good deal of unity among this small, rather tightly knit, group of bureaucrats, cattleowners, and politicians.

The potential conflict between this elite and the peasantariat in the longer run was secondary to the common necessity of creating a more secure economic base and capacity to act. In addition, the small size of the middle class and its limited income meant that its ability to "conspicuously consume," or to be believed to do so, was limited. Materially, it did not appear that the peasantariat was being exploited to support the affluence of the elite. For example, in 1975, only 500 households (out of 89,624) had incomes of P 8,690 (approximately $10,000) or more in rural areas. In 1976, only 1,077 wage-earning and salaried citizens earned P 300 ($360) or more per month out of a total of 50,676 wage and salary earners. In urban areas in 1976, only about 3 percent of the people had a yearly income of P 8,000 ($9,600) or more,[39] which accounts for the relatively modest life-style of most of the middle-class elite.[40]

The period from 1966 to 1974 was one of intense activity, but this activity can be characterized as a prologue, as a setting of the stage. The country's increased resources were used to create a foundation upon which future investments in production could take place, and the allocations appeared to be in the general interest, not in the interest of any particular class. Overall benefits were evident, if unequally dis-tributed, which sustained the political unity of the elite and reinforced its connection with the peasantariat. The electoral strength of the BDP in both 1969 and 1974 indicates this fact. The period was not devoid of political conflict—for example, there was the reduction in the power of the traditional authorities—but that conflict was managed so that it did not become predominant.

Most important, the changes that did take place rested on the maintenance or extension of existing social and political relations of production. Growth and increasing incomes did not require a change in the class structure of society; on the contrary, growth and increased incomes resulted from the extension of mining in Botswana and the distribution of the resulting revenues.

The prospect of future conflict, however, was implicit. Once the basic infrastructure was created and new incomes were absorbed, more class-specific outlooks would emerge. The peasantariat needed agricultural assets and increasingly secure wages and conditions of work in wage employment. The emerging elite needed private ownership of land for cattle production and the maintenance of low-wage employment. The possibility of conflict was therefore high.

Consolidation and New Initiatives: 1975–1980. By 1975, the primary physical infrastructure was in place or in the process of being constructed. The completion of this phase, which I shall call consolidation, raised two important issues for the developing political economy. One was the issue of what new directions should be undertaken in terms of allocating resources to productive purposes, including the allocation of resources to various class-specific purposes. The second was how to manage the sociopolitical strains that would be created by this new phase of development.

The debate on allocating resources to production outside of mining focused on agriculture, and within agriculture, on beef production. This interest was understandable. Because of the importance of cattle to the national economy, and the facts that the control of cattle was in the hands of the governing elite and that cattle production was also critical to the peasantriat, it was this sector of the economy that provided the most material link between the two classes.

The ecological issues of overgrazing and the chaotic state of water development highlighted the necessity for reforms. However, the solution, the tribal grazing lands policy (TGLP), was more the result of the class base of cattle ownership and control than of the technical constraints the policy was created to solve.[41] The irreconcilable problem concerning the cattle industry was that the interests of the minority of the people, those who owned medium- and large-scale herds, and the majority, those with no or few cows, were contradictory. The development interests of the former lay in having secure rights to land and water, which would give them exclusive control over these factors of production. This control, in turn, would create the long-term possibility of capitalization and the ability to organize labor in the most rational way—in the direction of wage labor. The majority, the peasantariat, required secure cattle assets, individually or collectively, and the right to land and water. Their needs concerning production and asset distribution contrasted with the needs of the cattleowners.

As the TGLP was carried out, these differences became apparent. Initially, it was thought that the peasantariat could be persuaded to accept the changes on the assumption that everyone would benefit by them. A land-use planning exercise and other research revealed, however, that no change could meet the needs of all classes. First, it was found that the land that was "easily occupiable has for the most part already been occupied" and that on eastern tribal lands, "new boreholes . . . would be sufficient in number to provide cattleposts for only the biggest owners still in communal areas." The conclusion was that far from opening up the land for new peasantariat cattle production, "not enough animals will be moving off the communal range to alleviate the overgrazing problem."[42]

It was also found that unexpectedly large numbers of people already lived on cattlepost lands that were destined to be zoned as commercial areas. Although many of these people worked for cattlepost owners, many also used the land themselves. From the point of view of the cattlepost owners, such people were surplus labor and would have to move.[43]

Limited evidence suggests that the peasantariat was not completely satisfied with the rural development agenda in general and unenthusiastic about the TGLP in particular. In a 1974 survey, nearly half the peasantariat (but slightly less than one-quarter of the rural well-to-do) said that government had made no difference in their lives since independence. Only 29 percent of the peasantariat, but 42 percent of the well-to-do, said that government had helped a great deal in their having a more comfortable life.[44] Concerning the TGLP, radio learning-groups that were formed as part of the process of public consultation were very skeptical about the benefits of the program. "Throughout the campaign . . . many questions asked if and how the poor would benefit from TGLP. In the first three report forms this was consistently one of the main themes. The poor and those with no cattle were not satisfied by social justice statements in the policy, and were questioning government about what was going to happen to them."[45]

Although the process of zoning land was slowed down by such concerns, it continued, and by 1980, it was clear that modifications would have to be made—but these would essentially be in the direction of benefiting the commercial farmers. They would not be required to fence land, restrict herd size, or pay an onerous rent, but they would secure exclusive use of the land. Given the composition of the elected political leadership and the agrarian interests of some of the civil servants, the modifications were not surprising.[46]

Nevertheless, great caution was required for three reasons. First, the physical dispossession of the peasantariat, a drastic increase in overcrowding in communal areas, or new limits on the peasantariat's access to draft animals could deprive a large number of people of a portion of their subsistence, which would probably cause large-scale and spontaneous outright opposition. Second, blatant moves in such a direction would finally undermine the social relationships of rural production, which provided a critical political link between the cattle-owning political elite and the peasantariat base. Finally, dispossession would have the effect of causing new demands not only for jobs (which would be expensive to create) but also for significantly higher wages. Basing the calculation of urban minimum wages on the average rural

TABLE 5.4
Urban Working Class and Salariat Wages per Day, 1974–1980

Year	Salariat[a]		Working Class[b]	
	Minimum	Maximum	Minimum	Maximum
1974	P11.13	P34.39	P2.00	P6.66
1976	13.51	41.26	2.40	7.95
1978	18.88	57.13	2.70	8.10
1980	23.12	69.46	4.10	10.14

[a] The salariat includes people with a degree entering
the administrative ranks of the public service directly as
well as people who entered the lower grades and have been
promoted.
[b] The ranges are for industrial-class people in the
public service.

Sources: Botswana, Directorate of Personnel, Personnel
Directive No. 26 of 1976 (Gaborone, 21 May 1976), pp. 12,
16, and 34; Botswana, Report of the Third Salaries Review
Commission (Gaborone: Government Printer, 1978), pp. 96,
98, and 108; and Botswana, Report of the Fourth Salaries
Review Commission (Gaborone: Government Printer, 1980),
Tables 1, 2, and 8.

income made the continuation of rural production necessary for some
proportion of peasantariat subsistence as urban wage policy depended
on the labor reserve political economy's being based on its rural and
agricultural sector. If that essential base were eliminated, the whole
rationale for low urban wages would disappear.[47]

For the urbanized peasantariat, this last problem was not important,
for workers in town consistently argued for higher wages. Strikes in
Orapa, Selebi-Phikwe, and Gaborone in the early and mid-1970s indicated
a certain militancy, as did demonstrations by unskilled workers at various
times.[48] The Department of Labour, for example, handled 455 grievances
between July 1976 and July 1977, two-thirds of which had been made
by unskilled workers, and a majority of these grievances were about
wages.[49]

Part of the problem, of course, was that although the working-
class wages were linked to rural income, the wages and salaries of the
people whose jobs had no rural counterpart were not. Hence, the
disparities in income persisted and widened during the period. Table
5.4 shows changes in wages and salaries from 1974 to 1980. Although
both sets of wages and salaries increased by more than 100 percent,
except for the working-class maximum, the absolute incomes showed
drastic, persistent differences. The differentials between the minimum
salaries and the minimum wages marginally increased from 1:5.56 to

1:5.63. Clearly, civil servants did well during the period, but the working class remained low on the wage scale.

This whole trend required that ways be found to manage the strains that it created, ways other than the occasional use of coercion as in the cases of the Selebi-Phikwe and bank workers' strikes. Unions were thought to be the answers, and by 1978, there were eleven unions covering virtually all sectors except agriculture; total membership was approximately 5,722. Four of the unions in the public sector accounted for nearly 54 percent of the total membership; the central government and parastatal workers alone accounted for 45 percent. However, at most, only 20 percent of the eligible workers joined a union, and even in Selebi-Phikwe, it was found that only 29 percent of the people eligible were actually members of the union in 1977.[50]

From the point of view of workers, organizing effective trade unions was not easy. Unions had to be organized on a sectoral basis, and 25 percent of the eligible workers had to vote for a union to establish any branch. Officers had to be citizens, and there was no closed shop. In addition, a 1974 amendment to the trade union law dictated that no supervisory personnel, on any level, could be members of the same union as the workers they surpervised, which meant that sometimes two unions were formed in the same establishment.[51]

Yet the government insisted on dealing with all unions as one element when negotiating wages. Therefore, after a lengthy period, the Botswana Federation of Trade Unions (BFTU) was formed in 1977, and it was led primarily by bank workers and diamond sorters, two rather privileged groups in the working class. The BFTU was then made responsible for negotiating agreements on labor policies, even though the federation was exceedingly weak, relying primarily on a volunteer staff and the assistance of the African American Labor Center.[52]

The weakness and division evident in the union movment contrasted with the central organization and strength of the employers' organization, the Botswana Employers' Federation (BEF). This group was open to all employers regardless of the nature of their activity. Annual subscriptions were sufficient to employ a full-time executive director and an assistant, pay secretarial and clerical expenses, rent comfortable offices in Gaborone, and pay the cost of circulating a newsletter. Noncitizens could hold office, and throughout most of the 1970s, the executive director was an expatriate. The BEF was represented on numerous government councils, boards, and committees, and it informed prospective members that "nothing of significance which concerns the field of employment is now decided without the involvement of the B.E.F."[53]

Despite all the problems, the use of mild administrative and coercive means meant that the country remained relatively calm.[54] These actions, combined with the basic acquiescence of the rural peasantariat and the signs of material progress, were sufficient to keep the country united. Despite some fears that the conflicts of the period might stimulate a drift toward the opposition, the BDP won handily in the 1979 elections.

During the 1975–1980 period, the main sociopolitical consequences of the mineral-led strategy emerged. The country's partnership with multinational mining companies produced enormous resources, and these resources became the basis for a rapid growth of the national economy, including public services of all kinds. This growth rapidly expanded both working-class and elite positions so that by 1980, far more Botswana citizens were employed in Botswana than in South Africa.

A condition of this growth was the maintenance of the rural household base combined with the wage and union policies. The effect of these policies was not only to continue the peasantariat but to extend that class in the national economy. Whereas formerly, wage-employed members of the peasantariat had been mainly an external phenomenon, they now became part of the predominant internal pattern. The national migration study found that 29 percent of the labor force members were migrants and 21 percent were migrants in Botswana. More to the point, 79 percent of the rural dwelling units had a wage worker present or absent, and less than 25 percent of the rural units relied solely on agriculture. The income of 36 percent of the rural units relied on a combination from three sources—arable agriculture, livestock production, and wages; 26 percent had incomes from a combination of wages and either arable agriculture or livestock; and 10 percent had incomes from wages alone.[55]

The sizable elite, or petty bourgeoisie, that controlled the government developed on this base, and it was in its interest to maintain the pattern. Hence, during the period, resource allocations were heavily oriented toward services and benefits that were not predominantly in the interests of the poor in rural areas or the low-wage-earners in urban areas.

However, long-term problems also began to be evident during this period. Conflicts in the rural areas began to develop as the TGLP began to erode the base of household production, and urban wage policies also became persistent sources of conflict. In other words, class divisions generated during the period of growth began to require much more direct management than formerly. The political problems implicit in these divisions, and within the elite as its different elements sought to develop, were projected into the post-1980 period.

Fissures and Fractures: 1980–1983. The early 1980s were characterized by a process of fissure and fracture in the political economy. Coinciding with the death of Seretse Khama in 1980, a number of implicit development tendencies became apparent and made changes in tactics, if not strategy, necessary. The political unity of the governing coalition became less cohesive as the limits of infrastructural development were reached and the revenues from the mineral exploitation were absorbed. Revenue stabilized, and demands increased. The consequences were serious, if ambiguous, particularly for the working class.

The need for new initiatives was highlighted by Michael Lipton's thorough and meticulous analysis of employment and labor use.[56] It discussed the deteriorating international economic situation, including a long-term decrease in Botswana's ability to export labor to South

Africa because of restrictions in that country. The report was also highly critical of further infrastructural development that was unrelated to directly productive activities. Lipton argued that unless significant changes were made, the problems of unemployment and underemployment would worsen. If that situation occurred, any further development of the classes that had increased and benefited from the previous plans would be forestalled and the conditions of the vast majority of the people would become worse.

Lipton's solution was a form of populist competitive capitalism. He argued for a redistribution of the agricultural assets (primarily cattle) in order to provide opportunities for work and a greater, if minimal, degree of peasantariat self-sufficiency in the rural areas. In addition, he argued for the relaxation or elimination of regulations and restrictions on urban and rural commercial and industrial activities combined with lower urban minimum wages. The effects of these suggestions would be to "free" the market: creating, on the one hand, outlets for profitable investment and, on the other hand, wage employment opportunities for the rapidly urbanizing peasantariat that was unable to engage in direct agricultural production.

Such solutions were politically naive. The large cattleowners were not likely to give up their ownership of cattle, even if they were handsomely compensated, unless they could have guarantees of a continuation of peasantariat labor and loyalties. Such guarantees were not part of the Lipton scheme, so his main recommendation died in the cabinet.

On the other hand, the crisis outlined by Lipton and some of his solutions did attract attention. Something did have to be done. The report also provided new and powerful arguments for encouraging Batswana entrepreneurship in commerce and the use of state subsidies for that purpose, as well as arguments for direct investment by the state in productive activities rather than in infrastructure.

The social basis for new initiatives lay in the emerging class configuration and the material position of the earlier periods. The completion of the basic infrastructure led to discussions of its utility for specific activities, and there could also be discussion as to the uses of revenues, generated by mining and beef exports, that exceeded what was needed for recurrent costs. The prospect of an expansion of such revenue from mining at Jwaneng made even more possibilities for allocations of social resources possible.

At the same time, differences began to develop in the elite group. The career public servants needed to secure the economic base of the state's revenues, and they felt that continuing the partnership with the sources of external (mainly South African) capital in the mines, brewery, hotel, and other businesses would accomplish this goal. For other public servants, the more complex economy offered the possibility of moving to employment in the private sector or going into private business, including agriculture. A new range of commercial and light manufacturing businesses, often with mixed citizen-foreign ownership, made this pos-

Trading stores in Mahalapye.

sibility attractive. Some senior members in the public service therefore retired or resigned to join the private sector, which began a process of closer cooperation between the two sectors. Finally, there continued to be a great deal of talk about low morale in the civil service, much of it apparently related to the fact that other elite elements were gaining ground at the expense of government employees.

Public servants continued to enjoy regular salary and fringe benefit increases, although at a reduced rate. Adjustments were made in 1981 and 1982, including a substantial widening of a guaranteed car-loan scheme,[57] and the 1980 Salaries Review Commission even argued that increasing public service salary scales was actually a form of social welfare and rural development. The peasantariat fabric of society was noted in the argument that "a considerable amount of the incomes earned in the urban areas is spent on relatives in the rural areas," and it was also argued that urban salaries result in rural investments in cattle, arable farming, and housing construction, which the committee felt "creates employment in the rural areas and helps ward off the tide of migration to the urban areas."[58] However, there were still the same low minimum standards of income for the peasantariat and no increase in that class's ability to engage in production.

Outside the public service, the small but growing professional and business groups began to see a future in commercial investments. Using the Lipton report, these people argued for a relaxation of restrictions, a redirection of resources away from infrastructure, and a decrease in the proportion of development funds allocated to large-scale farming. In addition, they were critical of the foreign presence in commerce and industry and argued for government programs that would support citizen commercial ventures as opposed to noncitizen ones.[59] Although some of these people were interested in establishing new agricultural ventures, others wished to begin or expand businesses or engage in lucrative housing speculation.

Such business activity was much in evidence during this period. The mushrooming of small general dealerships, bars, and bottle stores was dramatic. Larger investments were also made (a motel and a bar/restaurant/nightclub in Gaborone, for example), and there was also a greater range of joint ventures with foreign businessmen. Transportation businesses such as taxi and small bus companies also expanded. Housing construction and the attendant renting and speculative activities exploded. Although this type of activity was most evident in the rapidly expanding urban areas, it was also true in the major villages.

The demand for assistance was recognized in 1982 with the establishment of the financial assistance policy, which initially set up a 5-million-pula fund to assist new businesses. New ventures outside of the cattle industry that had significant employment and import-substituting opportunities could qualify for subsidies, which would "raise the rate of profit on these new ventures during the first five years of operations."[60] Thus, people could more easily enter business because they would be assured of the state's assistance.

Large-scale cattleowners' demands for public resources were undiminished, the TGLP continued, and there were new initiatives in arable farming. The allocation of land and the creation of individual rights for large commercial ranches continued to be primary activities, and by the end of 1981, nearly 9 percent of the total surface area of the country had been zoned as commercial, including a large percentage of the available, readily usable grazing land. Despite protestations to the contrary and a renewed concern about the problems of the small farmers, commercial ranch zoning and planning became the major focus of the TGLP, which raised questions about the circumstances under which some of the ranches were allocated. In addition, provisions of the TGLP concerning stocking limitations and the "one man, one ranch" rule were dropped, which undermined the ecological and social equity arguments that had been primary in the original drafting of the policy.[61]

The resulting dislocation of the rural population stimulated the creation of several communal service centers, which were allocations of communal land in commercial areas where the displaced peasantariat could live and be available as a rural working force. Such centers were not created smoothly, and the displaced people sometimes resisted their dispossession.[62]

Developments in arable agriculture were similar. The "land grab" of the late 1970s[63] resulted in a new arable lands development policy (ALDP), but it only assisted the process because it provided material inputs such as inexpensive loans for implements and fencing. Although, like the TGLP, the program was supposed to improve the ability of the very small farmers to produce crops, the ALDP appeared to be of most advantage to those people who could, because of land holdings and resources, use such inputs—i.e., the medium- and large-scale farmers.[64]

All of the demands of each section of the elite were slightly different to the point of being competitive. The earlier unanimity of the class, which had been rooted in its small, largely undifferentiated character and the common need for an infrastructure, no longer necessarily prevailed, and each faction needed to generate arguments and political support in order to ensure a favorable, or at least not a harmful, allocation of resources.

Given these circumstances and the death of Seretse Khama, it is not surprising that a good deal more political competition developed. Because of his background and preeminent political position, Seretse Khama had symbolized the unity of the Batswana social classes and their governing elite. His passing exposed the facts that this unity was somewhat fragile and that this fragility was the result of developments that had occurred in the political economy of Botswana.

This political situation is too recent to place in a long-term perspective, but its major outlines may be indicated. Although a smooth transition took place, there was and continues to be a great deal of debate about the long-term viability of unity in the cabinet, party, and nation. President Masire lacks the automatic political base Seretse Khama had in the peasantariat and among the elite and on those grounds alone, the possibility of political disruption exists. The government's insistence that Khama's picture be replaced by one of Masire on the walls of government offices and in other public places, as well as on the currency, symbolizes Masire's weak position as well as providing political ammunition for his opponents, actual and potential. There is, additionally, the factor of Ian Khama, brigadier of the defense force and chief of the Bangwato, who may be seen by some people as the long-term legitimate successor to his father, Seretse Khama.

This fracturing of the elite has been manifested in a variety of ways on the political level. Rumors about a possible split in the BDP and the possibility of creating labor and social democratic parties, hotly denied officially,[65] have been persistent, and there has been speculation about factions in the cabinet that are led by ministers with presidential ambitions. In response to these rumors, the BDP reorganized in 1981 and created a more centralized structure for the party.[66] However, at least in mid-1982, the impression was that the local BDP officials were less than enthusiastic about any such assault on their control of their constituencies.[67]

The outcome of all these changes in the early 1980s is not a foregone conclusion. The patterns of growth and class development will continue, but their consequences will depend upon how their effects are managed. The maintenance of the peasantariat base in the rural areas combined with a continued growth in mining may permit a smoothing over of the divisive tendencies. On the other hand, a stabilization of growth might stimulate the competition for resources and worsen the position of the peasantariat and the elite in urban and rural areas. Such a situation could open the door to political mobilizations around ethnic and other regional factors and thus result in an uncertain political situation.

6

Botswana in the World: Diplomacy of a Frontline State

Botswana's domestic underdevelopment at independence was paralleled by its international situation. The country did not have the material resources to operate a far-flung network of embassies or a strong internal foreign relations establishment. It had few sources of information on international issues beyond the mass media, no cadre of experienced diplomats, and no well-developed foreign policies.

Yet the need to generate international resources required that an international relations infrastructure be created. Moreover, Botswana's room for maneuver in southern Africa, specifically in its relations with South Africa and rebellious Rhodesia after 1965, demanded that Botswana have international visibility. As long as Botswana was engulfed in a network of minority-ruled states, it had to develop an international position if it were to maintain its independent status.

From independence in 1966 to the present, Botswana has attempted to develop an international position that would facilitate its domestic development as well as its ability to play a regional role within a world context. The development of a political and administrative capacity to formulate and execute foreign policies has been evident, as has the selective development of diplomatic missions and foreign policies. In southern Africa, Botswana is a member of the Frontline States and a member of the Southern African Development Coordination Conference (SADCC).

BECHUANALAND/BOTSWANA IN A SOUTH AFRICAN ORBIT

Understanding the course of Botswana's international relations since independence requires a brief reference to the history of Bechuanaland. In the early nineteenth century, the foreign policy of the independent Tswana societies consisted of contact and accommodation with European

A Botswana–South Africa border post.

missionaries and traders. That policy essentially consisted of allowing the settlement of limited numbers of missionaries in the area and a state monopoly on the rules under which trade would be conducted. However, increasing pressure from Afrikaners and other European interests eventually led to the Batswana request for British protection, which was granted in 1885.

British protection guaranteed the continued existence of the Batswana states. From that point of view, the Batswana foreign policy in 1884/1885 was successful, but there was, of course, an enormous price to be paid for the protection. Initially, the price was the concession to the British South Africa Company (BSAC) of land for a railway and European settlement. In the longer term, the price was the acceptance of Bechuanaland's subordinate role in a region dominated by South Africa. Batswana states had no choice but to become members of the customs and monetary unions, accept the roles of being a supplier of labor to South Africa and a consumer of South African goods, and allow Britain's colonial administration to be centered on that country's relations with South Africa and Rhodesia. Such a price effectively prevented any independent foreign policy for Bechuanaland.

Although the protectorate's foreign policy was constrained, it did not disappear. The chiefs did manage to negotiate for British government rule instead of BSAC rule in 1895, and, as noted earlier, the Batswana were reasonably effective in resisting South Africa's demand for the incorporation of the protectorate.[1]

Still, the rather thoroughgoing transformation of the formerly independent Tswana societies into the labor reserve pattern of colonial Bechuanaland eliminated any truly independent foreign policy. The chiefs in Bechuanaland had to conform to British policy, which left little opportunity for independent action.

It was only in the early 1960s, as South Africa accepted the inevitability of independence for Bechuanaland, Basutoland, and Swaziland, that the development of an independent foreign policy emerged as an issue.[2] The issues were what policies and actions would protect and further Botswana's national development in a hostile regional environment and how to array the country's capacity to formulate policy and execute action.

INSTITUTIONALIZING INTERNATIONAL RELATIONS

When developing the institutions to formulate and execute foreign policy, the leaders had to take into account the country's limited resource base. The budget allowed for neither a far-flung network of missions abroad nor an elaborate external affairs establishment at home.

At independence, a small external affairs operation was established in the Office of the President, and three diplomatic missions were created abroad in London, Lusaka, and Washington, D.C. Soon thereafter, a separate mission was created in New York at the United Nations (UN). The Lusaka High Commission represented the country's point of contact with the rest of independent Africa, the high commissioner acting as "Botswana's roving ambassador in Africa."[3] The mission in London facilitated a continuing close relationship with Britain and allowed for diplomatic contact with European nations, although on a nonresident basis, and the New York mission gave Botswana a permanent presence in the United Nations. These missions attempted to maximize Botswana's visibility in world forums and in the two countries, the United States and Britain, that were seen as likely sources of significant aid.

By 1970, a number of countries had missions in Gaborone, notably Britain, Nationalist China, the United States, and Zambia—the last representing an important symbolic link with independent Africa. Botswana did not establish diplomatic relations with South Africa, preferring to coordinate any necessary activities through other means.

With the achievement of budgetary self-sufficiency, the external affairs section expanded, although modestly. In 1972, a secretary for external affairs and a full-time staff were appointed. No new missions were established, but Botswana's diplomatic contacts increased. The London High Commission was accredited to seven countries including Britain, the Washington embassy was accredited to Canada, and the Lusaka High Commission was accredited to five other African countries as well as to the Organization of African Unity (OAU). Nonresidential accreditation existed for Lesotho and Swaziland.[4] The External Affairs staff supporting this activity was small, consisting only of the secretary and three staff members.[5]

A minister for external affairs, A. M. Mogwe, was appointed in 1974 in recognition of the "increasing diplomatic contacts and the increasing need for high-level diplomatic representation at international meetings." In 1977, an embassy was opened in Brussels, largely because of the need to maintain access to the market for beef in the European

Economic Community. The Brussels embassy was also accredited to five other European countries.[6]

By 1980, ten countries had diplomatic missions in Botswana, including the United States, Britain, Zambia, Nigeria, Libya, the Federal Republic of Germany, the People's Republic of China (PRC), and the Soviet Union (USSR).[7] Overall, twenty-eight nations had accredited diplomatic representation.[8] In addition, Botswana was represented in a variety of international organizations.[9] This level of representation required expansion in the headquarters staff, and by 1981, the Department of External Affairs, now headed by a minister, had a staff of ten.[10]

Thus, Botswana has established a pattern of international contacts and developed an internal foreign policy establishment. Although exceedingly modest, the diplomatic missions were established to generate as much exposure in world affairs as possible, and certainly, Botswana has established diplomatic contact with its long-term aid donors and other African states.

On the other hand, given its limited resources, the small Department of External Affairs can never hope to compete—in research and intelligence and the formulation of policy—with the states to which its missions are accredited so most of Botswana's economic international relations are handled in other ways. For example, major agreements with aid agencies and foreign investors have been concluded through the Ministry of Finance and Development Planning and other ministries.

DIVERSIFICATION OF DEPENDENCE

In order to achieve the goals of domestic development and national independence in the southern African context, Botswana had to follow four "maxims" as Richard Dale puts it.[11] First, Botswana had to develop allies among the other black African states "so that it would not have to face its powerful neighbor alone." Second, Botswana had to avoid creating any impression that it condoned apartheid in South Africa. Third, it had to develop an international nucleus of aid to avoid relying on South Africa for material and manpower resources. Fourth, Botswana had to develop international visibility to prevent "any diplomatic and economic isolation that might result from being closeted next to South Africa in Southern Africa." These maxims involved two aspects of foreign policy formulation. One was the creation of an international position that would promote national development; the second was the creation of an orientation toward and policy on the issue of liberation in southern Africa.

The creation of an international position that would promote national development was based essentially on three assumptions. One was that although Botswana's underdevelopment had been created by its overwhelming dependence on South Africa, it would not be possible to completely disengage from those dependent relationships. In 1964, Seretse Khama observed that "quite frankly it must be recognized that our Territory is to a very large extent dependent on the Republic [of

South Africa] and that as much as possible a good neighbor policy towards the State must be fostered by the government and peoples of Bechuanaland for their own good."[12] But, second, national development required a lessening, or where possible an elimination, of that dependence, which made it necessary to develop relationships with other nations to create room for maneuver. "Botswana's objective is to diversify its external relations to the greatest possible extent."[13]

Third, it was assumed that the advanced capitalist countries would be the most compatible partners in Botswana's attempt to decrease its dependence on South Africa. The maintenance and extension of ties with Britain, for example, was desired "because Britain is a country which gives aid of a kind we need and in a way which is wholly acceptable to us."[14] As long as such relationships came "without political strings or unacceptable economic conditions,"[15] they were viewed as being within the framework of nonalignment and a means of achieving economic independence. The extension of such relations to other Western countries was viewed in a similar light.

Botswana's policy therefore was one of diversifying its dependence,[16] which, it was hoped, would both widen the pool of resources and reduce the extent to which Botswana had to rely on South Africa. Given the Botswana elite's commitment to an essentially free market form of development, the choice of Western countries to be the main source of resources was logical and was perceived to be based on the country's economic and political interests.

The development of Botswana's international relations has reflected these assumptions and perceptions, and the country's strategy has been reasonably successful. The creation of diplomatic missions in Western Europe and North America has provided essential and permanent means of contact and communication, and development aid and technical assistance have been forthcoming in quantities that are sufficient to allow Botswana to avoid requesting or accepting such aid from South Africa.[17] The building of a north-south road to Zambia was financed largely with funds from the United States, and the country's ability to begin taking over Rhodesia Railways in Botswana in the late 1970s depended not upon South African but other external support. The longer-term plan to achieve a greater transportation independence from South Africa by means of a railway to Walvis Bay when Namibia becomes independent has a similar external base.

Botswana's cultivation of relations with European countries has led to a more or less permanent access to the European market for Botswana beef, thus decreasing the country's dependence on the South African market. Such contacts also have made it possible for the Botswana Development Corporation (BDC) to seek foreign investors in countries other than South Africa, as was the case when Germans invested in the Prinz Brau Brewery. To the extent that growth has been the result of the generation of large, external non–South African resources, the policy of diversification has allowed such actions as the creation of an independent currency, and it has allowed Botswana to withstand economic pressures that South Africa might have brought to bear.

There are, of course, limits to and costs of such a policy. No amount of diversification can make it possible for Botswana to totally disengage from its connections with South Africa, as has been evident throughout the independence period. The Botswana economy continues to depend on the South African transportation system, and the bulk of the country's consumer goods continue to come from South Africa. South African capital continues to be the most significant in mining, and in the end, South African capital also displaced German capital in the brewery. In addition, South African investors became the BDC's major partner in the hotel and travel agency businesses.

There are other costs as well, especially the cost of becoming further integrated into an international system that is dominated by the advanced capitalist countries. This was the goal intended, and up to a point, this integration has increased Botswana's ability to develop its national economy. However, there is also the longer-term issue of whether or not this new permanent dependence can or will allow for a more or less unlimited form of national development.

ON THE FRONT LINE: BOTSWANA AND LIBERATION IN SOUTHERN AFRICA

The second, and not unrelated, aspect of Botswana's foreign policy has been how to relate to the cause of liberation in southern Africa. This aspect is related to national development in the sense that Botswana's development has always been seen in the larger context of the development of the nations around it and in the sense that the country's position as a nonracial alternative to racism in South Africa has increased the inflow of international resources.

It is worth recalling that at independence in 1966, except for the "technical border" with Zambia, Botswana was completely surrounded by the minority-ruled states of Rhodesia, South Africa and its colony, South West Africa. Botswana did not have the diplomatic, economic, or military capacities to confront South Africa, and the other independent African countries were in no position to defend Botswana from direct attack. Nor could those countries protect the economy of Botswana from retaliation by South Africa for whatever reason.

But, inescapably, Botswana had to stake out a position regarding minority rule in southern Africa. Not to do so might have given substance to the perception that Botswana was just another Bantustan. Not to do so would also have been to deny the strong belief of Seretse Khama and others in Botswana that majority rule and nonracialism were viable in southern Africa, and thus to also deny the liberal ideas of equality and democracy that were implicit in Botswana's polity.[18]

Botswana moved cautiously but inexorably in the direction of creating a foreign policy that would distance it from South Africa and rebellious Rhodesia without committing economic and political suicide.

The prospects of Botswana's fashioning a role for itself in the struggle for liberation improved with the independence of Angola and Mozambique in the mid-1970s, although the environment continued to be hostile and increasingly dangerous as South Africa shifted from its "outward reach" policy—cooperation with a "constellation of southern African states"—to policies of destabilization in the early 1980s.

Beginning before and continuing into the early independence period, Botswana expressed its views concerning South Africa and other minority-ruled states. Although Botswana had to develop a good-neighbor relationship with South Africa, it sought to distance itself from the system of apartheid in that country. Thus, at the first meeting after independence of the National Assembly, Seretse Khama said that a good-neighbor policy "is not to say that we approve of the racial policy of the Government of that country. It must be perfectly obvious from the nature of our policy in this country that the reverse is the case."[19] Subsequently, in the United Nations, the OAU, and other forums, Botswana has condemned the injustice of apartheid and insisted that it be eliminated, consistent themes of its foreign policy toward South Africa and the other minority-ruled states.

Yet Botswana has had to be exceedingly careful with regard to the specifics of this broad principle, such as the use of Botswana's territory by groups opposed to racial domination, the problem of refugees, international alliances, sanctions, and appropriate ways to bring about change. In its handling of these specific questions, the broad outlines of Botswana's foreign policy have emerged and been developed.

One element is nonalignment. Botswana will "align ourselves with any country or groups of countries if our conscience permits us to do so and if such relationships would benefit the people of Botswana."[20] Countries supporting Botswana's policy of nonracialism and arguing for change in southern Africa will be viewed as friendly and as possible allies on those issues. The effect of such alliances would be to build an international support network for Botswana in southern Africa.

Second, Botswana has adopted a policy of noninterference in "the internal affairs of other countries" and called for a reciprocal policy on the part of South Africa. "In particular we will not permit Botswana to be used as a base for the organization or direction of violent activities directed toward other states."[21] In addition to anything else, such a policy would not give South Africa or Rhodesia cause to invade Botswana on the grounds that Botswana allowed military operations to originate there.

On the other hand, Botswana will not shut its doors to "genuine political refugees." Such people will be given a safe haven as long as they refrain from planning or attempting "to achieve the violent overthrow of the Government of any country from within the boundaries of Botswana." Any refugees who engage in such actions "will do so at their own peril," and "appropriate action" will be taken against them by the Botswana government.[22]

Third, Botswana has consistently expressed its preference for peaceful, negotiated solutions to the problems of minority racial domination. "We disapprove, in fact condemn, the use of force as a means of settling international disputes. Instead, we believe that all differences and quarrels between nations can, and in fact should, be brought to conference tables for peaceful negotiation and solution."[23] Although consistently holding such a position, Botswana also recognizes that as a practical matter, there are circumstances under which it cannot oppose the right to resort to violence. Botswana will not "condemn those who resort to violence to gain freedom in such situations. . . . It is possible of course to be more or less skeptical about the chances of success of violent tactics in different situations. But that is a matter of political and military judgment and not of morals."[24]

Finally, Botswana's foreign policy addresses the question of sanctions—economic, political, and military—in southern Africa against Rhodesia or South Africa. On the one hand, Botswana recognizes the value of such sanctions. Discussing the Rhodesian situation in 1969, Seretse Khama noted that "the maintenance and intensification of sanctions . . . help to undermine the viability of Rhodesia as a white-ruled state," and he applauded the isolation of Rhodesia in the international community and established the principle for Botswana that sanctions can be an effective tool in trying to persuade an ostracized nation to change its ways.[25] But, at the same time, Botswana did not commit itself to full participation in the sanctions against Rhodesia, let alone the call for sanctions against South Africa, as Botswana felt that to do so would be to threaten its own independence. Therefore, Botswana has committed itself to imposing sanctions when doing so will not harm its own national development.[26]

Although limited by the fact that "Botswana was ill-equipped to assist in the promotion of African majority rule" in Rhodesia, South Africa, and Namibia,[27] Botswana's diplomatic and other activities have sought to translate this policy into action, and it has done so amid the unfolding of events in the region, including the independence of Mozambique and Angola in 1975, an intensified opposition to apartheid in South Africa in the early 1970s, and particularly the Soweto uprising in 1976 and Zimbabwe's independence in 1980. Botswana did so as well in the context of its own national economic growth in the 1970s.

Botswana's activities have had regional, continental, and world dimensions. Relations with Zambia have been carefully cultivated. An exchange of visits by Seretse Khama and Kenneth Kaunda, the opening of a Zambian High Commission in Gaborone, the building of a north-south road to Zambia, flights from Zambia to Francistown, and the persistent assertion of a common border symbolized by the Kazungula Ferry have all bound Botswana to Zambia and, by implication, to the other majority-ruled countries to the north. These activities have created a place for Botswana in the community of African countries that assert the right of people in southern Africa to be free of racial oppression.

Beyond Zambia, Botswana has also developed a close relationship with Tanzania, and there was a particularly close personal relationship between Seretse Khama and Julius Nyerere. Tanzania has wished to encourage whatever level of disengagement it could for states bordering minority-ruled states and has desired to create a united front in the region. Until 1975, the only countries that could be so encouraged with some effect were Zambia and Botswana. From Botswana's point of view, Nyerere is a powerful ally in the OAU and beyond, and he can strengthen Botswana's ability to have its case heard and supported. In particular, Botswana has benefited by Nyerere's position regarding the limits of action that can be expected of a country such as Botswana. "We can ask that they should do everything possible to assert the principle of human dignity. But we should not ask them to commit suicide."[28]

As events unfolded, these and other relationships developed. Although Botswana did not sign the 1969 Lusaka Manifesto, feeling unable to participate in what amounted to a call for sanctions, it associated itself with the manifesto, including endorsing it in the OAU and the United Nations. Botswana (but not Lesotho or Swaziland) is also a member of the Frontline States organization which, since 1976, includes Tanzania, Zambia, Botswana, Angola, and Mozambique.[29] As a frontline state, Botswana participated—at some risk—in the major collective endeavors to secure Zimbabwe's independence. Subsequently, Botswana has continued to play a role in the consultations and negotiations regarding Namibia and South Africa. In addition, Botswana has played a role at OAU meetings, emphasizing Botswana's position and soliciting the support of the OAU for its efforts.

Botswana's most recent regional involvement is with the SADCC. The secretariat of the organization is to be located in Gaborone, and Botswana has played a role in its meetings and deliberations. Although limited by its membership in the Southern African Customs Union, Botswana sees its participation in the SADCC as an alternative to a continuation of its dependence on South Africa.[30]

Beyond the region and the continent, Botswana's foreign policy has sought to generate sufficient visibility to ensure international support against any possible action South Africa or Rhodesia might take. It has also used Botswana's image as an exemplary democratic and nonracial state and society to generate resources that might reduce dependence on South Africa as well as stimulate the development of the national economy. The country's policy of harboring political refugees has secured aid for their maintenance, and the border incursions by Rhodesian troops and the creation of the Botswana Defence Force have attracted attention as well. Its diplomatic missions to European and North American countries, the United Nations, and the OAU have highlighted Botswana's position, and its diplomats have participated in negotiations to bring change to minority-ruled states.

Botswana's preference, particularly up to the mid-1970s, for allies in the West to support it on the question of liberation, as well as to support its national economic development, is worth noting. The Western nations were those with major interests in South Africa, Rhodesia, and Namibia, and closer relations with those countries, and their commitment to an independent Botswana in southern Africa, became a useful shield against South Africa. Botswana could call on the "conscience" of the West as well as on its resources.

By the mid-1970s, Botswana's international position was reasonably secure because of its connection with these Western nations, and the country began to develop useful contacts further afield. Botswana recognized the PRC in 1975, in lieu of Nationalist China, and also agreed to the establishment of an embassy by the USSR in the same year. Such relations, although bringing a hostile verbal reaction from South Africa, were seen as widening "our international relationships" and as indicating a desire "to maintain our credibility as a peace loving and non-aligned nation."[31] Although neither the PRC nor the USSR presence has resulted in any significant aid, the symbolism of their presence in Gaborone is important.

Botswana's relations with its racist neighbors have been affected by its policies and actions. Early on, Botswana provided a refuge for people fleeing Angola, and it also provided a safe haven for larger numbers of political refugees from South Africa after the Soweto uprising in 1976. In the latter stages of the war in Zimbabwe, several thousand refugees came across the border—so many that a camp had to be built to house them at Dukwe, northwest of Francistown. Botswana helped these refugees despite South African concern that the refugees were engaging in subversive activities in South Africa, and a certain amount of South African retaliation resulted, most notably the presumption of South African involvement in the assassination in Botswana of Abraham Tiro, a black South African student leader, by a parcel bomb in 1974.[32]

Botswana also imposed some limited sanctions against commerce with Rhodesia. Although some Rhodesian goods were available, including sugar to meet Botswana's needs, Botswana banned arms shipments on Rhodesia Railways in Botswana, ceased airline flights to Rhodesia, and banned the importation of Rhodesian beer and tobacco products.[33]

At the same time, Botswana has officially refused to sanction any military training or operations on its soil by members of liberation movements. It also has not allowed the liberation movements to have offices in Botswana, although representatives of these movements live more or less permanently in Botswana.

Refugees are also viewed with concern because their need for jobs, education, and sustenance represents a potential and significant drain on resources. They are also viewed as politically destabilizing, at times being blamed for internal problems, including a largely unsubstantiated claim that black South African students and staff fomented the "disturbances" at the university in 1976.[34] Nonetheless, refugees and others committed to liberation remain welcome within limits. The holding of a cultural festival in mid-1982 that centered around liberation, with the involvement of the African National Congress, shows that some liberation activity is allowed in Botswana.

Regarding relations with South Africa, Botswana has continued to refuse to establish a permanent mission in that country "until South Africa can guarantee fully that Botswana's representatives will in all respects, at all times, and in all places be treated in the same way as diplomats from other countries," conditions that would require South Africa to undergo significant internal change.[35] The contacts that are necessary to coordinate trade and political relations are managed on an ad hoc basis . Botswana has also refused to recognize the "independence" of the homelands created by South Africa for its African population, which has caused some difficulty as Botswana has a reasonably long contiguous border with one of those homelands, Bophutatswana.

However, Botswana's strong dependence on South Africa has continued. Batswana continue to migrate for employment there, although in smaller numbers than earlier. This decline has more to do with South African restrictions than it does with the supply of Batswana wishing to work. The importation of food and other consumer goods has continued, and the presence of South African business in Botswana, often in partnership with Botswana citizens, has increased throughout the postcolonial period.

BOTSWANA IN THE WORLD PERSPECTIVE

Four primary conclusions are suggested by this description of Botswana's international relations. One is that the country's limited resources have constrained Botswana's ability to develop an international network and a comprehensive foreign policy. Botswana has concentrated its resources in those places and on those issues where the resources would have the maximum effect from Botswana's point of view. The country's parsimonious location of missions in Africa, Europe, and North America illustrates this conservation of resources.

Second, a close relationship has been forged between the country's domestic development and international relations, and the essential conservatism of the internal economic and political mosaic has been reproduced in the international arena. Botswana's aid and diplomatic relations express a clear preference for the development of a market economy, and its preference for negotiation and compromise argues for moderate majority-rule governments rather than governments that are being made more radical because of revolution.

Third, Botswana's foreign policy has been reasonably successful from the government's point of view. The domestic economy has grown and, within limits, thrived, and Botswana has not been subject to systematic and persistent incursions of its territory or frequent South African retaliation. In the early 1980s, Botswana was not a consistent target for destabilization by South Africa, which contrasts with the apparent destabilization involving South Africa in Lesotho, Mozambique, Zimbabwe, and Angola and the regular assaults on African National Congress representatives in Swaziland.[36]

But, finally, Botswana's international relations raise three difficult issues for the future. First is the question of what is likely to happen in southern Africa. If Namibia achieves independence through a revolution dominated by the South West Africa Peoples' Organization (SWAPO), and if the African National Congress (ANC) is able to sustain and intensify its military activity in South Africa with the cooperation of neighboring states, Botswana's aloofness from the risks of armed struggle will be difficult to maintain. In other words, if the conflict becomes one of confrontation between South Africa and the states ringing that country, Botswana will have to choose between participating fully, and bearing the consequences of actual hostile action with South Africa, and remaining aloof, although its reasons for not participating fully would not have quite the validity they have had to date.

This possibility does assume that Mozambique, Zimbabwe, and Namibia would carry the liberation war to South Africa by opening their territories to liberation movements, but given their histories of armed struggle in achieving independence, such a commitment does seem probable if it were a concerted effort. Opening three or four fronts against South Africa might make victory possible, and certainly, South Africa's foot-dragging on Namibian independence and its participation in destabilizing actions in neighboring states indicate that South Africa is concerned about that possibility.

Second, there is the issue of Botswana's long-term prospects for diversifying its dependence. Although Botswana has more room for maneuver regarding South Africa than formerly, the price of this freedom has been more direct dependence on the advanced capitalist countries. Although the short-term gains might appear to make this price a small one, Botswana has reached the point at which one can question the long-term prospects for autonomous national development if the country continues to adhere to this policy. Alternatively, one can raise the issue of the extent to which this diversification has fixed Botswana on a trajectory that may not be in the long-term interests of the majority of its citizens.

Third, at the point at which real change, that is, majority rule, is likely in South Africa, one wonders what Botswana's policy will be. Its arguments and actions for an independent political and economic system have essentially presupposed white supremacy in South Africa. If South Africa had majority rule and a nonracial society, would not much of the logic of Botswana's national existence be undermined? Majority rule in South Africa would not eliminate the strength of the South African economy or its role as a regional magnet, and the economic argument for regional development centered on South Africa would be very strong. If a majority-ruled government in South Africa accepted a role for the private sector, Botswana would lose one of the main reasons why it has been able to generate the quantities of international aid and technical assistance it has relied, and continues to rely, on. Western donors would be likely to want an economically integrated southern African economy with South Africa as its core, and Botswana's foreign policy and international relations would probably be affected by this sobering reality.

7

Political Economy
of Botswana: Yesterday,
Today, and Tomorrow

Where is Botswana going? What is to be the likely outcome of its development? Such questions are dangerous to answer for two reasons. The obvious one is that an answer is unlikely to take into account all of the necessary elements, will be speculative, and will therefore probably be wrong. Second, the analytical framework of this book essentially says that the future is what emerges from class and political struggles, and hence, one cannot specifically predict it. Yet the question of the future needs to be asked, and an answer at least needs to be presented. A reasonable answer is to be found in a summary of the past and present development of the main outlines of class and political relations, in other words, in an assessment of the political economy of Botswana.

YESTERDAY: THE LABOR RESERVE IN HISTORY

The late-nineteenth-century mineral revolution in southern Africa, which was dominated by British capital and organized through an expanding British Empire, had a profound effect on African society. Precapitalist tributary societies became reserves of labor supplying an inexpensive labor force in the mining, and later the manufacturing, economy of South Africa. The labor was inexpensive because it was migratory, and an essential element of its subsistence continued to be directly produced by households in the tribal territories which, collectively, made up the Bechuanaland Protectorate. These circumstances led to the transformation of the mass of the population from being a more or less self-sufficient peasantry to being a peasantariat, a working class of a particular kind.

Political means brought about this transformation. The British colonial state imposed taxation and effectively created land shortages, and the introduction of new, manufactured household goods and food created the need for cash. These factors, combined with a lack of opportunities to earn cash in Bechuanaland (another effect of colonial policy), led large numbers of mainly adult males to seek work in South Africa. Their recruitment was facilitated by the colonial administration.

The political structure through which this transformation took place was indirect rule. Existing African political institutions were subordinated to the British colonial government even though their form and the political relations between the African chiefs and the peasantariat were retained. In other words, the purposes of existing economic and political relations were altered even though their form did not change. It was a short, but a crucial, step that changed the peasant who was ruled by traditional authorities to one of the peasantariat ruled by a colonial chief.

The consequences of this transformation were, however, enormous. Agriculture suffered because of a lack of male laborers, and women bore the brunt of agricultural production and family management. The effective integration of Bechuanaland into the South African economy stripped the African society in Bechuanaland of its autonomy. Political relationships were frozen in a rigid colonial and tribal form as the stability of the colonial polity relied on the patron-client relationship of a tributary society under the supervision of the colonial state. The working-class peasantariat did not become important politically because of the persistence of such relationships so its working life was effectively isolated from its political action.

However, the system was full of tension and contradiction, which, when combined with external changes around the time of the Second World War, led to nationalist political activity and independence. The poverty of the peasantariat, the tension between the chiefs and the colonial administration, the growth in the number of educated people who were necessary to maintain the system but were opposed to its continuation, and the creation of apartheid in South Africa created conditions in which a nationalist political movement could thrive. A coalition of teachers, cattleowners, clerks, and traditional leaders rather easily mobilized the peasantariat base around the demands for economic development and self-government. Independence in 1966 symbolized the strength of this movement, which had been organized through the Botswana Democratic party and led by Seretse Khama.

TODAY: DEPENDENT DEVELOPMENT

In important respects, achieving independence was a somewhat hollow victory. There was hardly a national economy so the government budget still had to be subsidized by Britain, and except for cattle production, there was only a limited agricultural productive capacity. The infrastructure of roads, schools, and other public services was rudimentary. The problems of development were immense, and the prospects were bleak.

From independence onward, a rather startling process of dependent development has taken place. It is dependent because it is made possible by foreign capital; it is development because the revenue generated from that alliance has stimulated class formation and has created dynamic processes of continuity and change in class relations.

Growth resulted from what was the second mineral revolution in Botswana, the discovery of valuable minerals in the country, particularly diamonds, and a reciprocal relationship was created between the government and mining investors to exploit the minerals. Mining capital provided the finance, management, and markets; the government created wage, tax, and other policies and practices; and the two groups divided the revenue.

The revenue accruing to the government allowed for not only the balancing of the national budget but also new investments. In addition, partially because of Botswana's economic growth, it became possible to attract considerable aid from abroad. The investment of these resources was mainly in infrastructure—in roads, schools, and health services— and in building a complex and effective national state.

The mineral-led economy and the investment of the resulting revenues brought about a process of class formation. Two such developments were apparent: the generalization of the peasantariat base and the widening and differentiation of an elite, or petty bourgeois, governing class.

With the exception of agriculture, the number of unskilled workers expanded rapidly in all sectors of the economy. The wage and benefit policies more or less ensured that these workers would come from the peasantariat and that because of low wages, that group would retain its rural base. That working-class peasantariat, including its rural component, is the most numerous class in Botswana. Although migration to South Africa has continued on a reduced scale, the national peasantariat predominates.

On this base, there has developed a small number of intermediary positions that are filled by people who have an adequate education and whose future lies in perpetuating the peasantariat base. The number of people filling these intermediary positions, as employees of the state or in the private sector, and the number of self-employed business people have expanded very rapidly. These people have joined with the existing political elite of cattleowners and senior civil servants to provide the leadership of government, party, and interest-group organizations.

Despite the juxtaposition of the peasantariat and the petty bourgeoisie, and through that of the peasantariat and mining capital, development has not led to political disorder. On the contrary, Botswana has maintained a competitive liberal-democratic party system, holding regular and open elections throughout the postcolonial period. The unity of the governing class and the maintenance of its popular base have prevailed despite the absence of any significant income redistribution and the strains of growth.

This unity has resulted from four facts. First, the governing class is unified on the issues of the need for a close alliance with mining capital, and the policies required to effect that alliance, and of the need to build a national infrastructure. Second, although the benefits of expenditures for such an infrastructure have been unequally distributed between the elite and the mass, everyone has received something. The peasantariat has jobs, better roads, and schools where there were none before. The perception of generalized benefits has led to acquiescence, which is not total but does exist in important respects. Third, underlying relationships on the land have been more or less maintained. There has been no generalized assault on the rural household base of the peasantariat, and although the resulting standard of living remains one of at least relative deprivation, the structural base has remained intact, which allows the elite to continue to have a necessary political connection with the peasantariat. Finally, the whole period has been one of more or less expanding resources. Mining continues to grow, and in addition, Botswana has been able to obtain a great deal of international aid. The country's position in southern Africa and its commitment to nonracialism have made it an attractive recipient for aid as the process of decolonization has continued—in the Portuguese territories, then Rhodesia, and now South Africa.

AND TOMORROW? PROBLEMS OF DEPENDENT DEVELOPMENT

The reasons for Botswana's growth and stability in the postcolonial period also imply that there will be a problem in sustaining dependent development in the future. They also illustrate the essential fragility and insecurity of such development.

Two observations show the main outlines of the problem. One is that the process of development that has taken place has not been based on and has not yielded actual control over the production that is its base. Receiving a significant share of the mining revenues is not the same thing as determining how, under what circumstances, and in whose interest mining will take place. Negotiated access to the protected European beef market is not the same thing as creating and managing cattle production so that that sector of the economy can grow independently. In its production, Botswana remains part of an international system over which it has no control. The country remains on the periphery of a world capitalist system, and in that system, its governing class remains an intermediary one.

Second, continued development along present lines will generate serious conflict. The peasantariat's struggle must be for absolute and secure rights to the means of agricultural production or wages that reflect the value of its labor. The petty bourgeoisie must struggle to secure its economic base as a salaried class and to extend its interests in developing production in the internal economy—in agriculture, commerce, and manufacturing. In doing so, the petty bourgeoisie faces the problem of permanent conflict with the peasantariat as existing petty bourgeois revenue depends on the peasantariat's current low wages and rural base. However, the interests of the politically important large-scale cattleowners and arable farmers are in securing exclusive land rights, a process that will have the effect of physical dispossession in rural areas, and such a process necessarily undermines the political connection between the governing class and the peasantariat. A consequence has been urban and rural peasantariat resistance. Strikes in the 1970s and urban demonstrations over wages are the most visible signs of this discontent. Although extraordinary and growing revenues from new mines can smooth over these conflicts, those revenues cannot eliminate the contradictions. One broad conclusion about the future therefore is that the primary contradiction in the structure of Botswana's political economy will continue to place limits on what can be done and will define political events.

Within that broad parameter, specific scenarios are difficult to predict. The condition of the world economy, the course of the struggle in South Africa, and the specific course of class struggles in Botswana will all determine what happens in that country. It is quite possible that postindependence policies can be maintained if mining revenues continue to grow and the process of dispossession is gradual. It may even be possible for wages to be increased sufficiently so that a more or less permanent urban proletariat can be created as well as a process of transforming agricultural labor into wage labor. Even so, given the nature of mining and Botswana's position, it is not likely that an autonomous national economy can be created.

On the other hand, there are signs that the present policy may not last. There are no guarantees that revenues will continue to increase, and even if they do, the petty bourgeoisie has shown a remarkable ability to consume increased resources. That group also has shown a propensity to use those resources to develop its activities in commerce and agriculture, and as a result, there has been much more conflict within the elite. This competition has focused on the use of state resources for cattle production, as salaries for the public servants, and for commerce and manufacturing. As the competition among the governing class intensifies, each faction will have to find some kind of popular base. It will not be possible for the governing class to mobilize the peasantariat in the interests of its own exploitation, so elements of the petty bourgeoisie will probably turn to ethnic and other regional issues to secure a following. The fracturing of political unity within the governing class and between it and the peasantariat could create a situation for political instability. Whether or not such instability would be resolved in the interests of the peasantariat is, of course, not certain.

What this discussion highlights, finally, is the significance of the peasantariat in the political economy of Botswana. It is the productive class as mining and cattle production depend on its labor, and it is also the critical class in the country's politics. It is therefore the crucial element in maintaining the coherence and the stability of the system.

The peasantariat is also very patient. During the 100 years of its existence, it has borne the brunt of development in southern Africa without receiving commensurate rewards. It has time and again given the benefit of the doubt, as well as its labor, to the people who control it, even when it is clear that the peasantariat has received the short end of the stick. For the most part, this patience has been based on the physical separation of the source of the peasantariat's livelihood (wage work in South Africa) and its household production (in Botswana) as its political life has been embedded in the latter, not the former.

This patience is not endless, however. Its end is not necessarily in sight, but as the peasantariat becomes a national class in Botswana, it is likely to undergo a political change. The people controlling its livelihood would be much closer than formerly, and the same people in the same place would control both the rural and the wage work elements of the peasantariat's livelihood. Such a condition might lead to some form of peasantariat political organization rather than a political organization with a peasantariat base and petty bourgeois leadership. What is clear is the fact that in these ways and for all of these reasons, the future of Botswana depends on the future of the peasantariat's relations with other classes—in Botswana and beyond.

Notes

CHAPTER 1

1. See H.C.L. Hermans, "Botswana's Options for Independent Existence," in Z. Cervenka, ed., *Land-Locked Countries of Africa* (Uppsala: Scandinavian Institute of African Studies, 1973), pp. 197–211.

2. Address to the twelfth annual conference of the Botswana Democratic party at Lobatse, 21 April 1973, reprinted in Gwendolen Carter and E. Phillip Morgan, eds., *From the Front Line: Speeches of Sir Seretse Khama* (London: Rex Collings, 1980), p. 157.

3. Hermans, "Botswana's Options," p. 210.

4. Botswana, *National Development Plan 1976–81* (henceforth cited as *NDP IV*) (Gaborone: Government Printer, 1977), table 1.3, p. 7, and *Statistical Bulletin* (Gaborone) 6:3 (September 1981), table 25, p. 37. The pula (P) was introduced on a par with the South African rand in 1976. For ease of presentation all currency is quoted in pula, even that predating 1976. The value of the currency before the pula was the same as the rand. Recent pula values have been as follows:

Year	One Rand/Pula Equals		
	$	£	SDR
1969–1971	1.40	0.57	
1973	1.44	0.59	
1975	1.36	0.58	
1977	1.19	0.68	
1979			1.0530
1981			.9931
1982	.95		

Sources: 1969–76: Penelope Hartland-Thunberg, <u>Botswana: An African Growth Economy</u> (Boulder, Colo.: Westview Press, 1978), p. xiii; 1977: Charles Harvey of the Institute of Development Studies, University of Sussex; 1979 and 1981: International Monetary Fund, <u>Balance of Payments Statistics</u> (Washington, D.C.), Vol. 32, pt. 1 (1981), p. 60, and Vol. 33, no. 6 (June 1982), p. 7; 1982: estimated.

5. International Monetary Fund, *International Financial Statistics Yearbook 1980*, (Washington, D.C., 1980), p. 117.

6. *Statistical Bulletin* 2:1 (March 1977), table 1, p. 1, and *Statistical Bulletin* 6:3 (September 1981), table 25, p. 37.

7. *Statistical Bulletin* 2:1 (March 1977), tables 8(a) and 8(b), p. 11, and *Statistical Bulletin* 6:3 (September 1981), tables 14(a) and 14(b), p. 23.

8. See P. M. Landell-Mills, "The 1969 Southern African Customs Union Agreement," *Journal of Modern African Studies* 9:2 (1971), pp. 263–282, and Percy Selwyn, *Industries in the Southern African Periphery* (London: Croom Helm/IDS, 1975).

9. Botswana, *Migration in Botswana: Patterns, Causes, and Consequences*, National Migration Study final report (Gaborone: Government Printer, 1982), vol. 1, p. 30. South Africa has been reducing the recruitment of labor in Botswana. The estimate of absentees in 1976/1977 was 65,000—see Christopher Colclough, "Some Aspects of Labour Use in Southern Africa—Problems and Policies," *IDS Bulletin* 11:4 (1980), table 1, p. 30. That issue of the *Bulletin* was titled *Southern Africa: The Political Economy of Inequality* and is a useful general reference. Unless otherwise noted, Botswana is used to indicate the country, Batswana refers to citizens of Botswana, and Tswana is a cultural adjective.

10. *NDP IV*, p. 15.

11. See Richard Weisfelder, "The Southern African Development Coordination Conference: A New Factor in the Liberation Process," in Thomas M. Callaghy, ed., *South Africa in Southern Africa: The Intensifying Vortex of Violence* (New York: Praeger Publishers, 1983), pp. 237–266.

12. H. J. Cooke, *The Problems of Drought in Botswana*, National Institute for Research in Development and African Studies, Documentation Unit, Working Paper no. 17 (Gaborone, 1978), p. 3.

13. J. G. Pike, "Rainfall over Botswana," *Proceedings of the Conference on Sustained Production from Semi-Arid Areas, Botswana Notes and Records*, Special edition, no. 1 (Gaborone, 1971), p. 69.

14. Cooke, "Problems of Drought," p. 10.

15. Pike, "Rainfall over Botswana," p. 69.

16. Rainfall figures and zonal distribution adapted from ibid., p. 73.

17. Seretse Khama, "Botswana: Developing Democracy in Southern Africa" (Address at the Dag Hammarskjöld Center, Uppsala, 11 November 1970); reprinted in Carter and Morgan, eds., *From the Front Line*, pp. 99–100.

18. Michael Lipton, *Employment and Labour Use in Botswana*, Final report, vol. 1 (Gaborone: Government Printer, 1978), pp. 34–35.

19. The 1966 and 1976 figures are from Botswana, *Report of the National Commission on Education* (Gaborone: Government Printer, 1977), table 1.1, p. 14. Later figures are from Botswana, *National Development Plan 1979–85* (henceforth cited as *NDP V*) (Gaborone: Government Printer, 1980), table 11.1, p. 225, and *Statistical Bulletin* 6:3 (September 1981), table 10, p. 15, and table 11, p. 16.

20. *NDP IV*, p. 135.

21. See Botswana, *A Study of Constraints on Agricultural Development in the Republic of Botswana* (Gaborone: Government Printer, 1974), p. 17. See also I. Schapera, *Married Life in an African Tribe* (1940; reprint ed., Harmondsworth, Eng.: Penguin Books, 1971), particularly pp. 114–115.

22. See Christopher Colclough and Stephen McCarthy, *The Political Economy of Botswana: A Study of Growth and Distribution* (Oxford: Oxford University Press, 1980), particularly pp. 110–138; Botswana, *A Study of Constraints*; Lipton, *Employment and Labour Use*; and C. Bond, *Women's Involvement in Agriculture* (Gaborone: Government Printer, 1974).

23. See Colclough and McCarthy, *Political Economy of Botswana*, pp. 139–163, and *NDP IV*, pp. 181–195.

24. See *NDP IV*, table 4.3, p. 199, and *Statistical Bulletin* 2:1 (March 1977), table 1, p. 1.

25. Further information can be found in *NDP IV*, p. 197; Hermans, "Botswana's Options"; and Colclough and McCarthy, *Political Economy of Botswana*, pp. 163–165.

26. Botswana, *Report on the Population Census 1971* (Gaborone: Government Printer, 1972).

27. The 1981 population figures are from *Statistical Bulletin* 6:3 (September 1981), pp. II and III.

28. *NDP IV*, pp. 4–5.

29. Botswana, *Report on the Population Census 1971*, table 2, and *Statistical Bulletin* 6:3 (September 1981), table 2, p. IV.

30. In 1971, 49.8 percent lived in villages, 24.6 percent lived on the "lands," 12.9 percent lived on cattle posts, and 3.1 percent lived on freehold farms (Botswana, *Report on the Population Census 1971*, table 4).

31. Although the large villages (Maun, Serowe, Mochudi, Molepolole, Kanye, Ramotswa, Mahalapye, and Palapye) had resident populations ranging from 6,000 to 18,000 people, "many additional people live there for part of the year, when the agricultural rhythm allows" (*NDP IV*, p. 70).

32. Botswana, *Report on the Population Census 1971*, tables 13.5 and 13.6, pp. 105–106. See also, P. M. Landell-Mills, "Rural Incomes and Urban Wage Rates," *Botswana Notes and Records* 2 (1970), pp. 79–85; Jack Parson, "Aspects of Political Culture in Botswana" (Gaborone: Department of Political and Administrative Studies, University College of Botswana, 1976), tables 10–12, p. 17; and Robert Hitchcock, *Kalahari Cattle Posts* (Gaborone: Government Printer, 1978).

33. Jack Parson, "Cattle, Class, and the State in Rural Botswana," *Journal of Southern African Studies* 7:2 (April 1981), p. 237.

34. Botswana, *The Rural Income Distribution Survey in Botswana 1974/75* (henceforth cited as *RIDS*) (Gaborone: Government Printer, n.d.). See also E. B. Egner and A. L. Klausen, *Poverty in Botswana*, National Institute of Development and Cultural Research, Documentation Unit, Working Paper no. 29 (Gaborone, March 1980).

35. See Botswana, *Poverty Datum Line for Urban Areas of Botswana* (Gaborone: Government Printer, 1976), and Botswana, *Employment Survey (August 1976)* (Gaborone: Government Printer, 1978).

36. *RIDS*, pp. 84–85.

37. Ibid., p. 80, and *NDP IV*, p. 37.

38. Concerning the whole area of inequality and its nature and consequences in Botswana see Jack Parson, "Through the Looking Glass: Inequality in Post-Colonial Botswana" (Paper presented at the Southeast Regional Seminar on African Studies, Atlanta, April 1981); for the global context see the World Bank, *World Development Report,1980* (New York: Oxford University Press, 1980), chap. 4, pp. 32–45; see also, *NDP V* and the Botswana Democratic Party, *Election Manifesto 1979* (Gaborone, n.d.).

39. See J. H. Proctor, "The House of Chiefs and the Political Development of Botswana," *Journal of Modern African Studies* 6:1 (1966), pp. 59–80.

40. Concerning local institutions see William Tordoff, "Local Administration in Botswana," pts. 1 and 2, *Journal of Administration Overseas* 12:4 (October 1973), pp. 172–184, and 13:1 (January 1974), pp. 292–305, and Botswana, *Report of the Presidential Commission on Local Government Structure in Botswana 1979*, vol. 1 (Gaborone: Government Printer, n.d.).

CHAPTER 2

1. Selected general references on the organization of Tswana societies and states in the precolonial period include I. Schapera, *A Handbook of Tswana Law and Custom* (1938; reprint ed., London: Frank Cass and Company, 1970); I. Schapera, *The Tswana*, pt. 3 of the southern Africa portion of the Ethnographic Survey of Africa series, ed. Daryll Forde (London: International African Institute, 1953); Thomas Tlou, "A Political History of Northwestern Botswana to 1906" (Ph.D. dissertation, University of Wisconsin-Madison, 1972); and Q. N. Parsons, "The Economic History of Khama's Country in Botswana, 1844–1930," in Neil Parsons and Robin Palmer, eds., *The Roots of Rural Poverty in Central and Southern Africa* (London: Heinemann Educational Books, 1977), pp. 113–143.

2. See, for example, articles by Geoff Cohen, Ron Pahl, and John Cooke and T. Baillieul, in *Botswana Notes and Records* 6 (1974).

3. See L. Ngcongco, "Origins of the Tswana," *Pula* (Botswana Journal of African Studies) 1:2 (1979), pp. 21–46. In this chapter precolonial autonomous but related groups are referred to as "Batswana societies"; the political organizations are referred to as "Batswana states." The eight Tswana societies are the Bangwato, Batawana, Bangwaketse, Bakwena, Bamalete, Barolong, Bakgatla, and Batlokwa.

4. See, for example, Thomas Tlou, "Servility and Political Control: Botlhanka Among the BaTawana of Northwestern Botswana ca. 1750–1906," in Suzanne Miers and Igor Kopytoff, eds., *Slavery in Africa: Historical and Anthropological Perspectives* (Madison: University of Wisconsin Press, 1977), pp. 367–390.

5. Samir Amin, *Unequal Development: An Essay on the Social Formations of Peripheral Capitalism* (New York: Monthly Review Press, 1976), p. 15.

6. For information on this period see Tlou, "Political History"; Parsons, "Economic History of Khama's Country"; J. Mutero Chirenje, *A History of Northern Botswana 1850–1919* (Cranbury, N.J.: Associated University Presses, 1977); Anthony Sillery, *Botswana: A Short Political History* (London: Methuen, 1974); and Anthony J. Dachs, "Missionary Imperialism—The Case of Bechuanaland," *Journal of African History* 13:4 (1972), pp. 647–659.

7. Concerning the "gold rush" see Henderson Tapela, "The Tati District of Botswana 1866–1969" (D.Phil. thesis, University of Sussex, 1976).

8. This account is based mainly on Sillery, *Botswana*, pp. 80–113.

9. For further information on the councils see Jack Bermingham, "Shaping Colonial Rule: The Bechuanaland Protectorate African Advisory Council" (Paper presented at the African Studies Association annual meeting, Baltimore, Md., 1978); Sillery, *Botswana*; Lord Hailey, *An African Survey Revised 1956* (1957; reprint ed., London: Oxford University Press, 1968), particularly pp. 498–505; K. D. Manungo, "The Role of the 'Native' Advisory Council in the Administration of the Bechuanaland Protectorate, 1919–1960" (B.A. dissertation, Department of History, University of Botswana and Swaziland, 1977); and M. M. Holela, "The Role of the European Advisory Council in the Administration of the Bechuanaland Protectorate, 1920–1960" (B.A. dissertation, Department of History, University of Botswana and Swaziland, 1978).

10. Quoted in Harold Robertson, "From Protectorate to Colony: The Constitutional Status of Bechuanaland, 1885–1936" (Paper given at the University College of Botswana, n.d.), p. 16. See also J. E. Spence, "British Policy Towards the High Commission Territories," *Journal of Modern African Studies* 2:2 (1964), pp. 221–247.

11. See, among other works, G. L. Gunderson, "Nation Building and the Administrative State: The Case of Botswana" (Ph.D. dissertation, University of California-Berkeley, 1970); Sillery, *Botswana*; Quill Hermans, "A Review of Botswana's Financial History, 1900–1973," *Botswana Notes and Records* 6 (1974), pp. 89–116; and P. M. Landell-Mills, "The 1969 Southern African Customs Union Agreement," *Journal of Modern African Studies* 9:2 (1971), pp. 263–282.

12. Hermans, "Review of Botswana's Financial History."

13. See Giovanni Arrighi, "Labour Supplies in Historical Perspective: A Study of Proletarianization of the African Peasantry in Rhodesia," in Giovanni Arrighi and John S. Saul, *Essays on the Political Economy of Africa* (New York: Monthly Review Press, 1973), pp. 180–234.

14. I. Schapera, *Migrant Labour and Tribal Life: A Study of Conditions in the Bechuanaland Protectorate* (London: Oxford University Press, 1947), p. 7.

15. Stephen Ettinger, "The Economics of the Customs Union Between Botswana, Lesotho and Swaziland, and South Africa" (Ph.D. dissertation, University of Michigan, 1974).

16. Parsons, "Economic History of Khama's Country," and "'Khama & Co.' and the Jousse Trouble, 1910–1916," *Journal of African History* 6:3 (1975), pp. 383–408.

17. Alan Best, "General Trading in Botswana, 1890–1968," *Economic Geography* (1970), pp. 598–612.

18. Great Britain, Colonial Annual Reports, *Bechuanaland Protectorate 1947* (London: Stationery Office, 1949), p. 7.

19. Charles Simkins, "Labour in Botswana," *South African Labour Bulletin* 2:5 (1977), p. 28.

20. Concerning this demand and what lay behind it see Martin Legassick, "Gold, Agriculture, and Secondary Industry in South Africa, 1885–1970," in Parsons and Palmer, eds., *Roots of Rural Poverty*, pp. 175–200.

21. *Mine Natives' Wages Commission Report* (1944), par. 309, quoted in Schapera, *Migrant Labour*, p. 204.

22. Schapera, *Migrant Labour*, pp. 32, 39, 115.

23. Compare Samir Amin, *Unequal Development*; Giovanni Arrighi, "Labour Supplies"; Roger Leys, "Lesotho: Non-Development or Underdevelopment: Towards an Analysis of the Political Economy of the Labour Reserve," in T. M. Shaw and K. A. Heard, eds., *The Politics of Africa: Dependence and Development* (London: Longman and Dalhousie University Press, 1979), pp. 95–129; and Harold Wolpe, "Capitalism and Cheap Labour-Power in South Africa: From Segregation to Apartheid," *Economy and Society* 1:4 (1972), pp. 425–456.

24. See Hermans, "Review of Botswana's Financial History."

25. Concerning these consequences see Schapera, *Migrant Labour*; see also David Massey, "Labor Migration and Rural Development in Botswana" (Ph.D. dissertation, Boston University, 1981).

26. *Peasantariat* is a term coined to embrace the attributes of this type of working class in colonial societies of the labor reserve type. It embraces the persistence of a *peasant* type of agriculture and society with the prole*tariat* attribute of working for wages, and it indicates the maintenance of certain coterminous economic and political rights and relations in traditional society alongside the dispossession and denial of political rights represented by taxation and the domination of the colonial state. The term was first used in Jack Parson, "The Political Economy of Botswana: A Case in the Study of Politics and Social Change in Post-Colonial Societies" (D.Phil. thesis, University of Sussex, 1979). See also Jack Parson, "The Trajectory of Class and State in Dependent Development: The Consequences of New Wealth for Botswana," *Journal of Commonwealth and Comparative Politics* 21:3 (1983), pp. 265–286.

27. Indicated in Hoyt Alverson, *Mind in the Heart of Darkness: Value and Self-Identity Among the Tswana of Southern Africa* (New Haven: Yale University Press, 1978).

28. See Sir Alan Pim, *Financial and Economic Position of the Bechuanaland Protectorate*, Command Paper 4368 (London: Stationery Office, 1933). Concerning the period see Spence, "British Policy," and I. Schapera, *Tribal Innovators: Tswana Chiefs and Social Change 1795–1940* (London: Athlone Press, 1970).

29. Much has been written about this issue, and the details need not be recounted. A comprehensive and useful bibliography on the issue is Q. N. Parsons, "The High Commission Territories, 1909–1964: A Bibliography," in *Mohlomi: Journal of Southern African Historical Studies* (Roma, Lesotho) 1 (1976), pp. 96–107.

30. I. Schapera, *Handbook*, p. 33.

31. An early example on which research has been done is the case of Simon Ratshosa (see Q. N. Parsons, "Shots for a Black Republic? Simon Ratshosa and Botswana Nationalism," *African Affairs* 73:293 [1974], pp. 449–459).

32. Schapera, *Handbook*, p. 33.

33. The Seretse affair achieved a certain level of notoriety, and a fair amount has been written about it. See Jack Halpern, *South Africa's Hostages: Basutoland, Bechuanaland, and Swaziland* (Harmondsworth, Eng.: Penguin Books, 1965), pp. 274–281; Sillery, *Botswana*, pp. 146–151; Gunderson, "Nation Building," pp. 201–206; S. M. Gabatshwane, *Tshekedi Khama of Bechuanaland* (London: Oxford University Press, 1961), pp. 22–28; and Mary Benson, *Tshekedi Khama* (London: Faber and Faber, 1960), pp. 163–172. Concerning incorporation see Richard P. Stevens, "The History of the Anglo–South African Conflict over the Proposed Incorporation of the High Commission Territories," in Christian P. Potholm and Richard Dale, eds., *Southern Africa in Perspective: Essays in Regional Politics* (New York: Free Press, 1972), pp. 97–109. Details of institutional changes are found in Sillery, *Botswana*, pp. 145–161; Halpern, *South Africa's Hostages*, pp. 261–333; and Richard Stevens, *Lesotho, Botswana, and Swaziland* (London: Pall Mall Press, 1967), pp. 141–161.

34. See R. Nengwekhulu, "The Origins of Political Parties in Botswana," *Pula* 2 (1979), pp. 47–76. The first recorded party was the Bechuanaland Protectorate Federal party, which appears to have been organized in 1959 and to have disappeared around 1962. It was not of any significance in the late colonial period. See also Robert H. Edwards, "Political and Constitutional Change in the Bechuanaland Protectorate," in J. Butler and A. A. Castagno, eds., *Transition in African Politics*, Boston University Papers on Africa (New York: Frederick A. Praeger, 1967), pp. 135–165.

35. A brief summary by Mpho of the party's founding and early program is contained in his oration at the funeral of Motsete delivered at Mahalapye on 15 December 1974 (in the University of Botswana Library).

36. Richard Stevens, *Lesotho, Botswana, and Swaziland*, p. 143.

37. Edwards, "Political and Constitutional Change," p. 149.

38. Ibid., p. 151.

39. Gunderson, "Nation Building," p. 335. Local-level vignettes concerning the founding of the BDP and its personnel are found in Adam Kuper, *Kalahari Village Politics: An African Democracy* (London: Cambridge University Press, 1970), pp. 54–55, and Richard Werbner, "Small Man Politics and the Rule of Law: Centre-Periphery Relations in East-Central Botswana," *Journal of African Law* 21:1 (Spring 1977), p. 29.

40. Data from W.J.A. Macartney, "The General Election of 1969," *Botswana Notes and Records* 3 (1971), table 1, p. 33.

41. See "BDP 1965 Election Manifesto" in W.J.A. Macartney, ed., *Readings in Boleswa Government*, vol. 1 (Roma: U.B.L.S. Printing Unit, 1971), pp. 200–207.

42. For an early description by Koma, see "The Botswana National Front, Its Character and Tasks," Botswana National Front Pamphlet no. 1, mimeographed (n.p., 1966).

CHAPTER 3

1. Hoyt Alverson, *Mind in the Heart of Darkness: Value and Self-Identity Among the Tswana of Southern Africa* (New Haven: Yale University Press, 1978), p. 1.

2. Membership in the National Assembly was increased from thirty-one in conjunction with a new delimitation of constituencies following the census in 1971 (see Botswana, *Delimitation Commission 1972* [Gaborone: Government Printer, 1972]). Specially elected members are nominated by the president, and there is provision for other nominations from elected members. The elected members vote on the nominations, and the top four are selected (see Botswana, *Constitution* [Gaborone: Government Printer], pp. 79–81). The Speaker is chosen by a vote of members and need not be a member of the Assembly. There is also a clerk, deputy clerk, and a small administrative and clerical staff. Members have only rudimentary office and secretarial facilities, which limits their ability to function.

3. Specially elected members appear to be chosen for a number of reasons. Some have been defeated in general elections, including the vice-president, now president, in 1969. Some are retired public servants who join the cabinet through special election. Others have been chosen for specific reasons; for example, the first two women in the Assembly were specially elected.

4. Botswana, *Constitution*, ART. 62(d), p. 47. The latter requirement arises since English is the official language of debate and legislation. This situation creates problems for potential candidates since the bulk of the population does not know English. It also limits the participation of some members who qualify but are not as fluent as others.

5. For example, motions on rent control and an investigation of the Ministry of Works and Communications.

6. The Affiliations Proceeding (Amendment) Act introduced by a private member (not a cabinet minister or assistant minister), G. G. Sebeso (BDP), proposed to facilitate the claims of unmarried mothers for child support from fathers, but it appears that the cabinet was divided on the desirability of the bill. The lengthy history of the bill is chronicled in *Parliamentarian* 57 (1976), nos. 2, p. 113, and 3, p. 189; 58 (1977), nos. 1, p. 50, and 3, p. 194; and 59:1 (1978), pp. 41–42.

7. Some aspects of the procedure of lawmaking and the legal institutional dynamics of legislation are discussed in C.M.G. Himsworth, "The Botswana Customary Law Act,

1969," *Journal of African Law* 16:1 (Spring 1972), pp. 4–18. A further reference concerning Parliament as an institution is W.J.A. Macartney, "Local Government and the Politics of Development in Botswana" (Ph.D. thesis, University of Edinburgh, 1978).

8. Botswana, *Constitution*, ART. 48 (1), (2). This stipulation is in effect unless the Constitution or an act of Parliament provides otherwise.

9. Ibid., ART. 51 (1–3). Given the small size of the National Assembly, the cabinet includes a large number of the members. In 1978, for example, the twelve ministers and two assistant ministers represented 45 percent of the total BDP contingent in the National Assembly and 39 percent of the total membership of the Assembly, including the Speaker and the attorney general.

10. Ibid., ART. 51 (1), (4).

11. Those specially elected are chosen by other members "from among persons who are not and have not been within the preceding five years actively engaged in politics" (see Botswana, *Constitution*, ART. 80 [2]). Four members are elected by and from among the subchiefs in the Chobe, Francistown, Ghanzi, and Kgalagadi Districts.

12. Ibid., ART. 89 (2) and ART. 86 (3).

13. See J. H. Proctor, "The House of Chiefs and the Political Development of Botswana," *Journal of Modern African Studies* 6:1 (1968), pp. 59–79.

14. The smallest elected council, six, is in Selebi-Phikwe; the largest, thirty-two, is in the Central District. Jwaneng will constitute a new town council when fully developed. Ex-officio members include the chief (where appropriate) and the district commissioner. A minority of members may be appointed by the minister of local government and lands, a power that has ensured a BDP majority in the few instances in which the BDP did not have an elected majority (see Macartney, "Local Government," for details). The nine districts are North West (Ngamiland), Ghanzi, Kgalagadi, North East, Central, Kgatleng, South East, Kweneng, and Southern. The four towns are Francistown, Gaborone, Lobatse, and Selebi-Phikwe.

15. See T. C. Luke, *Report on Localisation and Training* (Mafeking, South Africa: Bechuanaland Government, April 1966), pp. 17, 141.

16. Names and dates of institutional creation are from "The Creation of New Institutions: Ministries and Selected Government Departments, Public Corporations, Boards, Museums, etc., 1966/67–1976/77," report prepared by H. Dahl of the Central Statistics Office. The document was published by permission in D. L. Cohen and Jack Parson, eds., *Politics and Society in Botswana* (Gaborone: Department of Political and Administrative Studies, University of Botswana and Swaziland, 1976), pp. 179–180.

17. Botswana, *Employment Survey (August 1976)* (Gaborone: Government Printer, 1978), table 1, p. 4.

18. See Botswana, *Report of the Presidential Commission on Localisation and Training in the Botswana Public Service* (Gaborone: Government Printer, 1977), par. 16.27, p. 98, and *Statistical Bulletin* (Gaborone) 6:3 (September 1981), table 4, p. 4.

19. Data from Botswana, *Report of the Presidential Commission on Localisation*.

20. Ibid. The teaching service also had a heavy complement of expatriates in 1977. Twelve out of the thirty-six headmaster/principal/deputy posts were filled by expatriates. All 65 public officer teachers were expatriates, and there were 667 expatriate secondary school teachers. Less than 10 percent of the academic staff positions in the University in Botswana were filled by local citizens (see ibid., par. 7.13, p. 42).

21. *Address by His Excellency the President Dr. Q.K.J. Masire, to the 39th Annual Conference of the Botswana Civil Service Association: 10th December 1981, Kanye* (Gaborone: Government Printer, n.d.), par. 11.

22. This concern has been expressed frequently in Parliament and by the Botswana Civil Servants Association. Criticism has frequently been directed not only toward expatriate senior officials, but also toward senior officials, both European and African, who are naturalized citizens.

23. Botswana, *Report of the Presidential Commission on Localisation and Training in the Botswana Civil Service and the Government Statement on the Report of the Commission* (Gaborone: Government Printer, 1973), pp. 11–12.

24. "BDP 1965 Election Manifesto," in W.J.A. Macartney, ed., *Readings in Boleswa Government*, vol. 1 (Roma: U.B.L.S. Printing Unit, 1971), p. 202; italics in the original.

25. References to these changes include J. Jeppe, "Local Government in Botswana," in W. Vosloo, D. Kotze, and J. Jeppe, eds., *Local Government in Southern Africa* (Cape Town: H. & R. Academica, 1974), pp. 137–138; William Tordoff, "Local Administration in Botswana–Part I," *Journal of Administration Overseas* 12:4 (October 1973), pp. 172–184; Richard Vengroff, *Botswana: Rural Development in the Shadow of Apartheid* (Cranbury, N.J.: Associated University Presses, 1977); and Macartney, "Local Government."

26. Each group had two representatives on the land board.

27. By 1979, slightly more than half of the councils' annual maintenance budget was being met by central grants, and it was expected that this proportion would increase to 77 percent during the 1981–1985 planning period. In 1979/1980, the local government tax accounted for 64 percent of nongrant income (Botswana, *Report of the Presidential Commission on Local Government Structure in Botswana 1979* [Gaborone: Government Printer, n.d.], vol. 2, appendixes, pp. 106–108).

28. Botswana, *Laws of Botswana* (Gaborone: Government Printer, 1975), chap. 40:01, pp. 3 and 12.

29. See *Parliamentarian* 56:3 (July 1975), p. 185.

30. Quoted in Tordoff, "Local Administration," p. 182.

31. See Louis Picard, *Rural Development in Botswana: The District Administration and the Creation of District Development Committees, 1966–1973*, National Institute for Research in Development and African Studies, Documentation Unit, Working Paper no. 14 (Gaborone, 1977).

32. See Louis Picard, "District Councils in Botswana: A Remnant of Local Autonomy," *Journal of Modern African Studies* 17:2 (June 1979), pp. 285–308.

33. This trend has been particularly true since the 1974 Accelerated Rural Development Program demonstrated the ability of councils to implement development projects on the local level (see Robert Chambers, *Botswana's Accelerated Rural Development Programme, 1973–76* [Gaborone: Government Printer, 1977]).

34. See Botswana, *Report of the Presidential Commission on Local Government*, vol. 1, p. 2, and particularly the summary of recommendations.

35. Louis Picard with Klaus Endresen, *A Study of the Manpower and Training Needs of the Unified Local Government Service, 1982–1992* (Gaborone: Government Printer, 1981), p. iv.

36. Picard, *Rural Development in Botswana*, indicates this fact.

37. It will be recalled that the minister may use his power to ensure BDP majorities.

38. Botswana, *Report on the General Elections 1969* (Gaborone: Government Printer, 1970), pp. 58–84; Botswana, *Report to the Minister of State on the General Election, 1974* (Gaborone: Government Printer, n.d.), pp. 20–21; and Botswana, *Report to the Minister of Public Service and Information on the General Election, 1979* (Gaborone: Government Printer, n.d.), pp. 21–22.

39. See Botswana Democratic Party, *Constitution*, post-Congress draft (Gaborone, 1981). Previously, the structure was that of subbranch, branch, constituency, national congress, and executive committee.

40. See W.J.A. Macartney, "The Success of Seretse," *Africa Report* 19:6 (1974), pp. 11–13.

41. Notes taken at a public debate on the 1974 elections at the University of Botswana, Lesotho, and Swaziland (Botswana Campus), 11 November 1974, at which Mr. Morake, then minister of education, represented the BDP, and an interview with D. K. Kwelagobe, minister of public service and information, 16 November 1974.

42. K. P. Morake, who was himself once a primary-school headmaster, quoted in *Botswana Daily News*, 13 November 1974, p. 1.

43. Macartney, "Success of Seretse," p. 12. Domkrag is a word for a wagon jack and is the symbol of the BDP's "jacking up the nation."

44. John Holm, "Rural Development in Botswana: Three Basic Trends," *Rural Africana* (1972), pp. 80–92. See also Richard Werbner, "Small Man Politics and the Rule of Law: Centre-Periphery Relations in East-Central Botswana," *Journal of African Law* 21:1 (Spring 1977), pp. 24–39.

45. See D. L. Cohen, "The Botswana Political Elite: Evidence from the 1974 General Election," *Journal of Southern African Affairs* 4:3 (July 1979), pp. 347–370.

NOTES TO CHAPTER 4

46. See John Holm, "Rural Development and Liberal Democracy in Botswana," *African Studies Review* 25:1 (March 1982), pp. 83–102. In other respects I disagree with Holm, who argues that the allocation of resources has not benefited the peasantariat and has not been part of their political docility.

47. Christopher Stevens and John Speed, "Multi-partyism in Africa: The Case of Botswana Revisited," *African Affairs* 76:304 (July 1977), pp. 386–387.

48. Election reports, 1969, 1974, and 1979.

49. Ibid.

50. See "The Botswana National Front, Its Character and Tasks," Botswana National Front Pamphlet no. 1, mimeographed (n.p., 1966).

51. The seats were Kanye North, Kanye South, and Ngwaketse/Kgalagadi. Bathoen beat then-Vice-President Masire in Kanye South by a margin of 740 votes out of a total of 1,750 (see Botswana, *Report on the General Elections 1969*, pp. 55–56).

52. See Botswana, *Report to the Minister of State on the General Election, 1974.*

53. Freedom squares are open meeting places for political party rallies as distinguished from the *kgotla*, which is technically closed to political party meetings.

54. See Botswana, *Report to the Minister of Public Service and Information on the General Election, 1979.*

55. See, for example, the BNF response to the 1982 budget speech in *Botswana Daily News*, 15 March 1982, p. 3. See also the rather strident exchange of charges and countercharges between the BNF—in particular, its secretary-general, Mareledi Giddie—and the minister of public service and information, Daniel Kwelagobe, in *Botswana Daily News*, 22 April 1982, p. 1, 26 April 1982, p. 1, and 29 April 1982, pp. 1 and 3.

CHAPTER 4

1. The deficit grant financed 34 percent of recurrent expenditures in 1959/1960 and 45 percent in 1964/1965 (see Quill Hermans, "A Review of Botswana's Financial History, 1900–1973," *Botswana Notes and Records* 6 [1974], table 1, p. 113).

2. Computed from Botswana, *National Development Plan 1976–81* (henceforth cited as *NDP IV*) (Gaborone: Government Printer, 1977), table 1.3 and fig. 1.2, pp. 7 and 8. Not a single bank operated in Bechuanaland until 1951, and then only once-weekly services were offered in Lobatse by Standard and Barclay Bank branches in Mafeking, South Africa. Post office savings banks, operated by the Savings Bank of the Republic of South Africa, were started in 1952. By 1954, Barclay and Standard Banks had opened branches in Francistown and Lobatse (see Great Britain, Commonwealth Relations Office, *Bechuanaland Protectorate 1951* [Morija, Basutoland, n.d.], p. 24; Great Britain, Commonwealth Relations Office, *Bechuanaland Protectorate 1952* [Vryburg, South Africa: Pretorious Bros., n.d.], p. 15; and Great Britain, Commonwealth Relations Office, *Bechuanaland Protectorate 1954* [Mafeking, South Africa: Controller of Stores, 1955], p. 21). Even the annual reports were printed outside the territory.

3. *NDP IV*, table 6.6, p. 109, and fig. 6.4, p. 111.

4. Great Britain, Colonial Office, *Bechuanaland Protectorate Report for the Year 1963* (London: Stationery Office, 1965), p. 60.

5. Great Britain, *The Development of the Bechuanaland Economy*, Report of the Ministry of Overseas Development, Economic Survey Mission (Gaborone: Government Printer, November 1965), tables 1 and 2, pp. 3 and 4.

6. Cited in Botswana, *National Development Plan 1970–75* (henceforth cited as *NDP 1970–75*) (Gaborone: Government Printer, 1970), pp. 12–13.

7. Great Britain, *Development of the Bechuanaland Economy*, p. 4.

8. Great Britain, Colonial Office, *Bechuanaland Protectorate Report for the Year 1964* (London: Stationery Office, 1965), p. 23.

9. Great Britain, *The Development of the Bechuanaland Economy*, table 3, p. 5.

10. *NDP 1970–75*, table 2-1, p. 12.

11. Great Britain, *The Development of the Bechuanaland Economy*, table 3, p. 5.

12. *NDP 1970–75*, p. 13.

13. Figures reported in ibid., table 4.3, p. 40.

14. Ibid., p. 2.

15. Great Britain, *Bechuanaland Protectorate Report for the Year 1964*, p. 15.

16. Percentages computed from Great Britain, *The Development of the Bechuanaland Economy*, appendix 2, p. 133. In addition, between 1955 and 1960, loans totaling £ 1,075,250 were received. Eighty-one percent was spent on "housing for government staff," and 10 percent was used to develop telecommunications. See also Hermans, "Review of Botswana's Financial History," pp. 107–108.

17. Botswana, *Transitional Plan for Social and Economic Development* (Gaborone: Government Printer, 1966), pp. 6–7.

18. See P. M. Landell-Mills, "The 1969 Southern African Customs Union Agreement," *Journal of Modern African Studies* 9:2 (1971), pp. 263–282.

19. *NDP 1970–75*, introduction, and pp. 1–18.

20. Ibid., p. 17.

21. See *NDP IV*. Guarantees are found in Botswana, *Constitution of the Republic of Botswana* (Gaborone: Government Printer, n.d.), chap. 2, ART. 8, (1[b]), and (2). These provisions are "entrenched," requiring agreement of two-thirds of "all members of the Assembly" to change them (see ART. 90).

22. *NDP IV*, p. 198. This policy continued with the creation of the Bank of Botswana; its policy has been to place no restriction on transferring interest and dividends (see *Bank of Botswana Annual Report 1977* [Gaborone, 1977] and subsequent years).

23. See *NDP IV*, p. 198. See also the publication *Business Investment in Botswana*, published by the Botswana Development Corporation, and details compiled in Penelope Hartland-Thunberg, *Botswana: An African Growth Economy* (Boulder, Colo: Westview Press, 1978), appendix B, "Government Policy Toward Investment," pp. 97–120.

24. *NDP IV*, p. 183. The government considered a shareholding free of charge of 15 to 25 percent as "normally appropriate."

25. *NDP 1970–75*, p. 13.

26. Botswana, *National Policy on Incomes, Employment, Prices, and Profits*, Government Paper no. 2 (Gaborone: Government Printer, 1972), p. 5. See also D. Ghai, *A Long-Term Wages Policy for Botswana* (Gaborone: Government Printer, 1971). Contemporary discussions of these issues are found in Dudley Jackson, "Income Differentials and Unbalanced Planning—The Case of Botswana," *Journal of Modern African Studies* 8:4 (1970), pp. 553–563, and P. M. Landell-Mills, "Rural Incomes and Urban Wage Rates," *Botswana Notes and Records* 2 (1970), pp. 79–85.

27. Councils were created for construction, transport, manufacturing, wholesale and retail trade, and hotel and catering industries (see Christopher Colclough and Stephen McCarthy, *The Political Economy of Botswana: A Study of Growth and Distribution* [London: Oxford University Press, 1980], pp. 188–190).

28. Concerning policies regarding mining and labor see Botswana, *National Development Plan 1979–85* (henceforth cited as *NDP V*) (Gaborone: Government Printer, 1980), especially pp. 192–194, and 216–218.

29. Botswana, *Rural Development in Botswana*, Government Paper no. 1 (Gaborone: Ministry of Finance and Development Planning, 1972), pp. 2–3.

30. Seretse Khama, "Botswana: Developing Democracy in Southern Africa" (Address at the Dag Hammarskjöld Center, Uppsala, 11 November 1970).

31. Botswana, *Rural Development in Botswana*, p. 2. See also *Proceedings of the Conference on Sustained Production from Semi-Arid Areas, Botswana Notes and Records*, Special Edition no. 1 (Gaborone, 1971).

32. R. Chambers and D. Feldman, *Report on Rural Development* (Gaborone: Government Printer, 1973).

33. This discussion is adapted from Jack Parson, "Cattle, Class, and the State in Rural Botswana," *Journal of Southern African Studies* 7:2 (April 1981), pp. 236–255. See also Lionel Cliffe and Richard Moorsom, "Rural Class Formation and Ecological Collapse in Botswana," *Review of African Political Economy* no. 16 (1980), pp. 35–52.

34. Chambers and Feldman, *Report on Rural Development*, pp. 116–119.

35. Ibid., pp. 116 and 119.

36. Ibid., pp. 120 and 133–134.

37. Botswana, *National Policy for Rural Development: The Government's Decision on the Report on Rural Development by Dr. R. Chambers and D. Feldman*, Government Paper no. 2 (Gaborone: Government Printer, 1973), par. 46, p. 6, and par. 49, p. 7.

38. Botswana, *National Policy on Tribal Grazing Land*, Government Paper no. 2 (Gaborone: Government Printer, 1975), pp. 6, 11, 13, 14.

39. Ibid., p. 14.

40. Ibid., p. 7.

41. Ibid., p. 9.

42. *NDP IV*, p. 76.

43. Ibid., pp. 158 and 148.

44. Ministry of Agriculture, "Arable Lands Policy," (Paper G at the National District Development Conference, Gaborone, 1978), pp. 1–2; italics in the original.

45. Michael Lipton, *Employment and Labour Use in Botswana*, Final report, vol. 1 (Gaborone: Government Printer, 1978), p. iii.

46. Ibid., pp. iv–xxvi.

47. *NDP V*, p. xi.

CHAPTER 5

1. See Christopher Colclough and Stephen McCarthy in *The Political Economy of Botswana: A Study of Growth and Distribution* (London: Oxford University Press, 1980), p. 91. Both authors served as planning officers in Botswana. See also their description of the evolution of planning and expenditures, pp. 84–109.

2. David Jones, *Aid and Development in Southern Africa* (London: Croom Helm in association with the Overseas Development Institute, 1977), pp. 113–114.

3. Botswana, *National Development Plan 1979–85* (henceforth cited as *NDP V*) (Gaborone: Government Printer, 1980), pp. 53–54.

4. Proportions calculated from Botswana, *National Development Plan 1976–81* (henceforth cited as *NDP IV*) (Gaborone: Government Printer, 1977) table 1.6, p. 12, and Botswana, *Estimates of Recurrent Expenditures and Estimate of Revenue and Expenditure of the Development Fund of the Year 1976/77* (Gaborone: Government Printer, n.d.), pp. 159–215.

5. A description of the agreement and negotiations is contained in F. Taylor Ostrander (who was employed by American Metal Climax), "Botswana Nickel-Copper: A Case Study in Private Investment's Contribution to Economic Development," in J. Barratt, S. Brand, D. S. Collier, and K. Glaser, eds., *Accelerated Development in Southern Africa* (London: Macmillan, 1974), pp. 534–549. See also Keith Jones, *Financing the First Decade of Development: An Analysis of Botswana's Public Debt (1966–1976)*, National Institute for Research in Development and African Studies, Documentation Unit, Working Paper no. 13 (Gaborone, 1977), pp. 56–57, for details of loans and capital costs.

6. Ostrander, "Botswana Nickel-Copper," p. 545.

7. See Jones, *Financing the First Decade*, p. 57.

8. Botswana Roan Selection Trust, Ltd., "Preliminary Results for the Year Ended December 31, 1977, of the Company and Its Subsidiaries," *Rand Daily Mail*, 17 March 1978, p. 19.

9. Ibid. and *New York Times*, 30 June 1982, National Edition, p. 31.

10. *NDP V*, pp. 186 and 202.

11. The history of the mines and information about the 1980 revenues are from Louis Nchindo, "Diamonds in Botswana" (Unpublished report, Gaborone, 1981).

12. De Beers Consolidated Mines Limited, "Chairman's Statement," *94th Annual Report to 31st December 1981* (Kimberley, South Africa, April 1982), p. 5.

13. Data computed from *State of South Africa: Economic, Financial, and Statistical Yearbook for the Republic of South Africa* (Johannesburg: DeGama Publishers, various years); 1978 data from De Beers Consolidated Mines Limited, *91st Annual Report to 31st December 1978* (Kimberley, South Africa, April 1979), p. 22.

14. Computed from figures on group production in De Beers, *94th Annual Report*, p. 17.

15. Botswana, *Employment Survey (August 1980)* (Gaborone: Government Printer, 1981), table 1, p. 10.

16. *NDP V*, pp. 184–185.

17. See Nchindo, "Diamonds in Botswana"; R. Silitshena, *Mining and the Economy of Botswana*, National Institute for Research in Development and African Studies, Docu-

mentation Unit, Working Paper no. 8 (Gaborone, 1976); and the 1975 and 1976 annual reports of De Beers Consolidated Mines Limited (Kimberley, South Africa, 1976 and 1977).

18. *NDP IV*, p. 199, and *NDP V*, p. 203.

19. Computed from *NDP IV* and *NDP V*.

20. *Statistical Bulletin* (Gaborone) 6:3 (September 1981), table 4, p. 4, and table 25, p. 37.

21. See Botswana, *Employment Survey (February 1971)* (Gaborone: Government Printer, n.d.), p. 11, and Botswana, *Employment Survey (August 1980)*, p. 25. See also Charles Harvey, "Foreign Investment in Manufacturing: The Case of Botswana's Brewery," in Charles Harvey, ed., *Papers on the Economy of Botswana* (London: Heinemann Educational Books, 1981), pp. 209–219.

22. Development expenditures 1966/1967–1975/1976 are from *NDP IV*, table 1.6, p. 12; 1976/1977–1978/1979, from *NDP IV*, table 2.10, p. 48; 1979/1980–1984/1985 are "projected actual expenditure" from *NDP V*, table 3.3, p. 76.

23. Proportions computed from Botswana, *National Development Plan 1973–78*, pt. 1 (Gaborone: Government Printer, 1973), table 2.4, p. 31.

24. The categorization of these tables is an approximation based upon the judgment of the beneficiaries of development expenditures. In addition, Table 5.3 includes the projected expenditures to 1985, but economic difficulties in 1981 and 1982 probably reduced the rate at which expenditures have taken and will take place.

25. From *NDP V*, table 2.13, p. 34.

26. Recurrent budget data are from *NDP V*, table 2.17, p. 54, which is in 1979/1980 prices. Subsequent recurrent estimates were adjusted for inflation using the same inflation factor used in estimating the total estimated costs of the plan.

27. Data computed from Table 15, "Recurrent Expenditure, Exclusive of Lending/Borrowing Operations 1966/67 to 1976/77," in D. L. Cohen and Jack Parson, eds., *Politics and Society in Botswana* (Gaborone: University College of Botswana, 1976), p. 289; *NDP IV*, pp. 386–401; and *NDP V*, table 2.13, p. 34, all in current prices.

28. See Botswana, *Budget Speech 1982*, delivered to the National Assembly on 22 February 1982 (Gaborone: Government Printer, n.d.).

29. Botswana, *National Development Plan 1970–75* (Gaborone: Government Printer, 1970), table 1.1, p. 1. The 1972 and 1975 figures are from *Statistical Bulletin* (Gaborone) 5:4 (December 1980), table 5, p. 5.

30. Botswana, *Regulations Governing the Wages and Conditions of Work of the Industrial Class* (Gaborone: Government Printer, 1966), pp. 14–20; Botswana, *National Policy on Income, Employment, Prices, and Profits*, Government Paper no. 2 (Gaborone: Government Printer, 1972), appendix 3, pp. 1 and 6; Botswana, Directorate of Personnel, *Personnel Directive No. 26 of 1976* (Gaborone, 21 May 1976), pp. 12, 16, and 34.

31. Botswana, *The Rural Income Distribution Survey in Botswana 1974/75* (henceforth cited as *RIDS*) (Gaborone: Government Printer, n.d.), pp. 221, 223, and 84–85.

32. Ibid., p. 111.

33. Botswana, *A Study of Constraints on Agricultural Development in the Republic of Botswana* (Gaborone: Government Printer, 1974), pp. 4, 7.

34. *RIDS*, pp. 97–100.

35. Botswana, *Employment Survey (August 1976)* (Gaborone: Government Printer, 1978), table 5, p. 9, and Botswana, *Poverty Datum Line for Urban Areas of Botswana* (Gaborone: Government Printer, 1976).

36. The salariat was roughly the entering grade in the public service "administrative cadre," which overlapped with the "executive cadre."

37. Wage figures are from Botswana, *Regulations Governing the Wages and Conditions*; Botswana, *National Policy on Income*; and Botswana, *Personnel Directive No. 26*.

38. N. M. Campbell and J. Abbott, "Botswana's Primary School System: A Spatial Analysis," in Botswana, *Report of the National Commission on Education* (Gaborone: Government Printer, 1977), vol. 2, Annexes, tables 2, 4, 5, and 6, pp. 6–9, 6–11, and 6–13. Originally published by the Institute of Development Management (Gaborone, 1976).

39. *RIDS*, p. 80; Botswana, *Employment Survey (August 1976)*, and *NDP IV*, p. 37.

40. See, for example, Anthony Sillery, *Botswana: A Short Political History* (London: Methuen, 1974).

41. A complete history of the tribal grazing land policy is yet to be written. Articles concerning its formulation and impact include the following: Jack Parson, "Cattle, Class, and the State in Rural Botswana," *Journal of Southern African Studies* 7:2 (April 1981), pp. 236–255; articles in *Land Reform in the Making: Tradition, Public Policy, and Ideology in Botswana: Journal of African Law* 24:1 (Spring 1980), particularly Robert Hitchcock's "Tradition, Social Justice, and Land Reform in Central Botswana," pp. 1–34; Lionel Cliffe and Richard Moorsom, "Rural Class Formation and Ecological Collapse in Botswana," *Review of African Political Economy* 16 (1980), pp. 35–52; and Colclough and McCarthy, *Political Economy of Botswana*.

42. Quotations are from Botswana, Ministry of Finance and Development Planning, "Rethinking TGLP in Light of the Landuse Planning Exercise" (Paper F at the National District Development Conference, Gaborone, 1978), pp. 7–8.

43. Robert Hitchcock, "Meeting Communal Needs in Commercial Areas: Integrated Land Use Planning and the Communal Service Centre Concept" (Consultancy report no. 5 for the National District Development Conference, Gaborone, 1978), p. 5. See also Robert Hitchcock, *Kalahari Cattleposts* (Gaborone: Government Printer, 1978).

44. See Jack Parson, "Political Culture in Rural Botswana: A Survey Result," *Journal of Modern African Studies* 15:4 (1977), pp. 639–650.

45. Botswana, *Lefatshe La Rona—Our Land: The Report on the Botswana Government's Consultation on Its Policy Proposals on Tribal Grazing Land* (Gaborone: Government Printer, 1977), p. A4.03. Approximately 3,500 groups averaging sixteen members were organized. Each had a study guide and listened to programs explaining the policy. They could then submit questions by mail. About half of the participants owned twenty or fewer cows.

46. Hitchcock found that one-third of the water source owners he interviewed were civil servants, "some of whom had an important say over policy matters relating to the TGLP." The rent was about four thebe ($0.04) per hectare for a 6,400-hectare ranch with no rent payable for the first three years (see Robert Hitchcock, "Tradition, Social Justice, and Land Reform," pp. 18 and 21).

47. A general reference on these points is David Cooper, "An Interpretation of the Emergent Urban Class Structure in Botswana: A Case Study of Selebi-Phikwe Miners" (Ph.D. thesis, University of Birmingham, 1982).

48. For accounts of the strikes and labor policy generally see James Cobbe, "Wage Policy Problems in the Small Peripheral Countries of Southern Africa, 1967–1976," *Journal of Southern African Studies* 2:4 (October 1977), pp. 441–468; Nelson Moyo, "The Application of Incomes Policy in the Private Sector with Reference to the Strike of Bank Employees in 1974," in Charles Harvey, ed., *Papers on the Economy of Botswana*, pp. 196–208; and David Cooper, "The State, Mineworkers, and Multinationals: The Selebi-Phikwe Strike, Botswana, 1975," in P.C.W. Gutkind, Robin Cohen, and Jean Copans, eds., *African Labor History* (Beverly Hills, Calif: Sage Publications, 1978), pp. 244–277.

49. Interview at the Botswana Department of Labour, 14 April 1978.

50. Ibid., and Nelson Moyo, "Draft Report on Industrial Relations at BCL, Selibi-Phikwe," mimeographed (University College of Botswana, 1977), p. 20.

51. See Jack Parson, "The Working Class, the State, and Social Change in Botswana," *South African Labour Bulletin* 5:5 (January 1980), pp. 44–55, and Nelson Moyo, "Some Aspects of the Trade Union Law in Botswana," *Pula* 1:1 (June 1978), pp. 171–175.

52. Trade union organization and the federation are more extensively discussed in Jack Parson, "The Political Economy of Botswana: A Case in the Study of Politics and Social Change in Post-Colonial Societies" (D.Phil. thesis, University of Sussex, 1979), particularly pp. 309–311.

53. BEF form letter to prospective members, revised March 1978, issued by John Price, executive secretary, p. 1. See also N.D.A. Hardie, "Chairman's Annual Review Presented at the Sixth Annual General Meeting" (Holiday Inn, Gaborone, 23 February 1978), and Parson, "Political Economy," pp. 308–309.

54. Other instances of coercion include the disturbances at the university in 1976 and 1978, discussed in Parson, "Political Economy," pp. 330–337.

55. Botswana, *Migration in Botswana: Patterns, Causes, and Consequences*, National Migration Study final report (Gaborone: Government Printer, 1982), vol. 1, pp. 2, 5, 37; vol. 3, p. 563.

56. Michael Lipton, *Employment and Labour Use in Botswana*, Final report (Gaborone: Government Printer, December 1978).

57. See *Address of His Excellency the President Dr. Q.K.J. Masire to the 39th Annual Conference of the Botswana Civil Service Association: 10 December 1981, Kanye* (Gaborone: Government Printer, n.d.). The scheme had advanced money for 460 officers at a cost of P 2,855,464. At the same time, the president cautioned public officers "not to hold the rest of society to ransom because the rest of society expects to be catered for by Government through the very resources often demanded exclusively by public officers" (par. 16).

58. Botswana, *Report of the Fourth Salaries Review Commission* (Gaborone: Government Printer, 1980), par. 1.13 and par. 1.24, p. 4.

59. For one clear expression of these ideas see D. N. Magang (lawyer and member of Parliament), *A Look at Botswana's Future Economic Prospects*, Speech made before the Botswana Society on 11 August 1981 (Gaborone: Printing and Publishing Co. Botswana [Pty.], n.d.). See also the contribution of the attorney general to the debate on the financial assistance policy reported in the *Botswana Daily News*, 14 April 1982.

60. Botswana, *Financial Assistance Policy*, Government Paper no. 1, approved by the National Assembly on 13 April 1982 (Gaborone: Government Printer, 1982), pp. 1–2.

61. See Botswana, Ministry of Agriculture, Rural Sociology Unit (TGLP Monitoring), *Tribal Grazing Land Policy 1981 Programme Review* (Gaborone, 1982), pp. 3 and 10. See also Botswana, *Report of the Commission of Inquiry into Ngwaketse First Development Area Ranches and Government's Decision on the Recommendations of the Commission* (Gaborone: Government Printer, December 1981). Other developments in cattle marketing confirmed the advantage of large farmers. The agreement to build a northern abattoir and the defeat in Parliament of a bill to more closely regulate cattle marketing are examples (see *Botswana Daily News*, 24 August 1981, p. 1, concerning the bill).

62. Botswana, *Tribal Grazing Land Policy 1981 Programme Review*.

63. First noted in 1978 in Botswana, Ministry of Agriculture, "Arable Lands Policy" (Paper G at the National District Development Conference, Gaborone, 1978).

64. See, for example, Botswana, Ministry of Agriculture, *ALDEP: Evaluation & Outreach, 1981* (Gaborone: Ministry of Agriculture, Division of Planning and Statistics, January 1982). See also E. B. Egner and A. L. Klausen, *Poverty in Botswana*, National Institute of Development and Cultural Research, Documentation Unit, Working Paper no. 29 (Gaborone, March 1980).

65. For example, see *Botswana Daily News*, 17 and 24 March 1981.

66. See Botswana Democratic Party, *Constitution*, post-Congress draft (Gaborone, 1981).

67. Interviews with BDP leaders in May 1982.

CHAPTER 6

1. See Richard P. Stevens, "The History of the Anglo-South African Conflict over the Proposed Incorporation of the High Commission Territories," in Christian P. Potholm and Richard Dale, eds., *Southern Africa in Perspective: Essays in Regional Politics* (New York: Free Press, 1972), pp. 97–109.

2. See Richard Dale, "Botswana," in ibid., pp. 110–124.

3. Botswana, *National Development Plan 1970–75* (Gaborone: Government Printer, 1970), p. 125.

4. Botswana, *National Development Plan 1973–78*, pt. 1 (Gaborone: Government Printer, 1973), p. 319.

5. Botswana, *Central Government Directory* (Gaborone: Government Printer, 1972), p. 2.

6. Botswana, *National Development Plan 1976–81* (Gaborone: Government Printer, 1977), pp. 249–250.

7. Botswana, *National Development Plan 1979–85* (Gaborone: Government Printer, 1980), p. 288.

8. Richard Dale, "Botswana's Foreign Policy: State and Non-State Actors and Small Power Diplomacy," (paper presented at the annual meeting of the African Studies Association, Philadelphia, 1980), p. 17.

9. See Botswana, *National Development Plan, 1979–85*, p. 288. The plan also proposed the expenditure of P 700,000 for new diplomatic missions, although their locations were unspecified. No new missions had been established by 1983.

10. Botswana, *Central Government Directory* (Gaborone: Government Printer, 1981), p. 118.

11. Dale, "Botswana," pp. 113–114.

12. Seretse Khama addressing the third annual conference of the Bechuanaland Democratic party in 1964, in Gwendolen Carter and E. Phillip Morgan, eds., *From the Front Line: Speeches of Sir Seretse Khama* (London: Rex Collings, 1980), p. 8.

13. Ibid., p. 86.

14. Ibid.

15. Ibid., p. 85.

16. See Sheridan Johns, "Botswana's Strategy for Development: An Assessment of Dependence in the Southern African Context," *Journal of Commonwealth Political Studies* 11:3 (November 1973), pp. 214–230.

17. Carter and Morgan, eds., *From the Front Line*, p. 87.

18. In this context, it is worth noting that even a cautious distancing of Botswana from South Africa could be perceived as threatening to the latter. "It is frequently forgotten that liberalism [equal individual political rights] in Southern Africa is in the mind of the Nationalist Party a revolutionary philosophy" (Willie Henderson, "Independent Botswana: A Reappraisal of Foreign Policy Options," *African Affairs* 73:290 [January 1974], p. 41). This conclusion highlights the 1948 assertion of Dr. N. Diedrichs (a minister in the South African government in the 1970s) that "this doctrine of liberalism that stands for equal rights for all civilised human beings—is almost the same as the ideal of communism" (ibid., p. 41).

19. Presidential address to the first meeting of the first session of the first National Assembly, 6 October 1966, in Carter and Morgan, eds., *From the Front Line*, p. 15.

20. Ibid.

21. Ibid., pp. 15–16.

22. Ibid., p. 16.

23. Seretse Khama, address to the Botswana Democratic party annual conference in 1968, ibid., p. 26, and statement on southern Africa at the Commonwealth Heads of Government Meeting, Singapore, 20 January 1971, ibid., p. 115.

24. Ibid.

25. Seretse Khama addressing the Council on Foreign Relations, New York, September 1969, ibid., p. 61.

26. See Seretse Khama's discussion of sanctions in his address to the ninth annual conference of the Botswana Democratic party in 1970, ibid., particularly pp. 89–90.

27. Dale, "Botswana's Foreign Policy," p. 10.

28. Nyerere in a speech to the Tanganyika African National Union (TANU) Conference in 1967, quoted by Seretse Khama at the ninth annual conference of the Botswana Democratic party, in Carter and Morgan, eds., *From the Front Line*, p. 90. The relationship between Khama and Nyerere is illustrated by the fact that Nyerere wrote a foreword for the collection of Khama's speeches.

29. For some aspects of the frontline situation see Carol Thompson, "Southern Africa: Frontline Challenge to the World Capitalist System" (Paper presented at the annual meeting of the African Studies Association, Philadelphia, 1980).

30. See Richard Weisfelder, "The Southern African Development Coordination Conference: A New Factor in the Liberation Process," in Thomas M. Callaghy, ed., *South Africa in Southern Africa: The Intensifying Vortex of Violence* (New York: Praeger Publishers, 1983), pp. 237–266.

31. See address by the president to the fourteenth annual conference of the Botswana Democratic party in 1975, in Carter and Morgan, eds., *From the Front Line*, p. 196.

32. The Dukwe camp was again being occupied by Zimbabwean refugees in 1983 because of the activities of "dissidents" in southwestern Zimbabwe. Concerning Tiro's

death see *South Africa: Time Running Out*, Report of the Study Commission on U.S. Policy Toward Southern Africa (Berkeley: University of California Press, 1981), p. 179.

33. See address by Seretse Khama to the ninth annual conference of the Botswana Democratic party in 1970, in Carter and Morgan, eds., *From the Front Line*, p. 90.

34. Botswana, *Report of the Commission of Inquiry Into Student Unrest at the University College of Botswana* (Gaborone, May 1977). In addition, the Botswana Defence Force raided some refugee homes, and the government banned an academic conference on liberation (see Tony Hodges, "Botswana: External Threats and Internal Pressures," *Africa Report* 22:6 [November-December 1977], p. 41).

35. Seretse Khama addressing the Council on Foreign Relations, in Carter and Morgan, eds., *From the Front Line*, p. 60.

36. This involvement includes the car bomb murder of the African National Congress (ANC) representative and his wife in Manzini in mid-1982. South Africa is known, or is believed, to be involved in supporting an antigovernment group in Lesotho. The South African military has raided ANC houses in Maseru, which has caused the deaths of Basotho civilians as well as ANC members, and the South African government supports the Mozambique resistance movement; has had military personnel in Zimbabwe; and supports the dissident Movement for the Total Independence of Angola (UNITA), in that country.

Selected Bibliography

Sources on the political economy of Botswana remain sparse and uneven in quality and coverage. This bibliograhy selects readily available primary and secondary works, which, taken together, provide more depth to the themes developed in the text.

PREINDEPENDENCE PERIOD

Chirenje, J. Mutero. *A History of Northern Botswana 1850–1919*. Cranbury, N.J.: Associated University Presses, 1977.
    Describes aspects of precolonial Tswana society and the impact of colonialism, particularly the effect of missionaries. Based largely on missionary documents.
Edwards, Robert H. "Political and Constitutional Change in the Bechuanaland Protectorate." In Butler, J., and Castagno, A. A., eds., *Transition in African Politics*, pp. 135–165. New York: Frederick A. Praeger, 1967.
    Describes institutional changes and the rise of political parties in the period immediately preceding independence.
Hermans, Quill. "A Review of Botswana's Financial History, 1900–1973." *Botswana Notes and Records* 6 (1974):89–116.
    Painstaking compilation and description of data on sources and totals of government revenues and functional expenditures.
Parsons, Q. N. "The Economic History of Khama's Country in Botswana, 1844–1930." In Parsons, Neil, and Palmer, Robin, eds., *The Roots of Rural Poverty in Central and Southern Africa*, pp. 113–143. London: Heinemann Educational Books, 1977.
    Excellent brief analysis of the precolonial Bangwato kingdom, its growth in the late precolonial period, and the effect of colonialism in subordinating and reorienting African society.
Schapera, I. *A Handbook of Tswana Law and Custom*. 1938. Reprint. London: Frank Cass and Company, 1970.
    A meticulous, primary descriptive survey of traditional Tswana society.
————. *Migrant Labour and Tribal Life: A Study of Conditions in the Bechuanaland Protectorate*. London: Oxford University Press, 1947.
    A description and analysis of the history, causes, and effects of the migration of labor to South Africa.
————. *The Tswana*. London: International African Institute, 1953.
    Vivid analysis of the precolonial social and economic life of Tswana society and the disruption caused by the development of colonialism.
————. *Tribal Innovators: Tswana Chiefs and Social Change 1795–1940*. London: Athlone Press, 1970.
    Analysis of the creative responses of African leaders to the colonial situation.

Sillery, Anthony. *Botswana: A Short Political History.* London: Methuen, 1974.
    A useful survey of events leading to the declaration of the protectorate. Also
    contains an account of nationalism but is rather weak on the independence period.
Spence, J. E. "British Policy Towards the High Commission Territories." *Journal of Modern
    African Studies* 2:2 (1964):221–247.
    Describes British colonial policies of parallel and indirect rule and the question of
    South Africa's attempts to incorporate Bechuanaland.
Tlou, Thomas. "A Political History of Northwestern Botswana to 1906." Ph.D. dissertation,
    University of Wisconsin-Madison, 1972.
    Relying on oral history and Schapera, gives an account of the nature of the Batawana
    polity in the late precolonial and early colonial periods.

CONTEMPORARY SOCIETY AND ECONOMY

Alverson, Hoyt. *Mind in the Heart of Darkness: Value and Self-Identity Among the Tswana
    of Southern Africa.* New Haven: Yale University Press, 1978.
    An inquiry into Tswana culture and society by examining the self-identity of people.
Bond, C. *Women's Involvement in Agriculture in Botswana.* Gaborone: Government Printer,
    1974.
    Survey-based description and analysis of the role of women in agriculture highlighting
    their central but subordinate position.
Botswana, Republic of. *A Study of Constraints on Agricultural Development in the Republic
    of Botswana.* Gaborone: Government Printer, 1974.
    Reviews obstacles to agricultural development and highlights the unequal distribution
    of assets for production as well as climatic problems.
_____ . *The Rural Income Distribution Survey in Botswana 1974/75.* Gaborone: Gov-
    ernment Printer, 1976.
    Results of a year-long national survey of sources of income and activity of rural
    households; contains excellent data on ownership of cattle and income distribution.
_____ . *Report of the National Commission on Education.* 2 vols. Gaborone: Government
    Printer, 1977.
    Thorough review of changes in education including access to education and policy
    recommendations; second volume contains supporting papers that include data and
    discussions of specific issues.
Cliffe, Lionel, and Moorsom, Richard. "Rural Class Formation and Ecological Collapse in
    Botswana." *Review of African Political Economy* 16 (1980):35–52.
    Reviews changes in rural society and economy in the colonial and postcolonial
    periods, particularly cattle production.
Colclough, Christopher, and McCarthy, Stephen. *The Political Economy of Botswana: A
    Study of Growth and Distribution.* London: Oxford University Press, 1980.
    Two former economic planners in Botswana survey postindependence changes by
    economic sector and raise issues of planning and income distribution.
Harvey, Charles, ed. *Papers on the Economy of Botswana.* London: Heinemann Educational
    Books, 1981.
    Collection of fifteen papers surveying economic changes and issues; written by
    economists and planners who have a great deal of experience with Botswana.
Lipton, Michael. *Employment and Labour Use in Botswana.* 2 vol. Gaborone: Government
    Printer, 1978.
    Meticulous and thorough review of the pattern of economic change in the inde-
    pendence era with recommendations for changes in policy to generate wage- and
    self-employment.

CONTEMPORARY POLITICS AND CHANGE

Botswana, Republic of. *National Development Plan 1970–75, 1976–81, and 1979–85.* Gaborone:
    Government Printer, 1970, 1977, and 1980.

Compilation of available data, review of past plans, and statements of present and future direction of development policy. More reliable and candid than is usually the case in development plans.

_____ . *National Policy on Tribal Grazing Land.* Government Paper no. 2. Gaborone: Government Printer, 1975.

Policy statement outlining the tribal grazing land policy as the centerpiece of rural development policy.

_____ . *Migration in Botswana: Patterns, Causes, and Consequences.* National Migration Study final report. 3 vols. Gaborone: Government Printer, 1982.

Report of a national multiyear study of external and internal migration with data, analysis, and recommendations.

Chambers R., and Feldman, D. *Report on Rural Development.* Gaborone: Government Printer, 1973.

Government-sponsored analysis of rural development policy, which subsequently became the basis for policy in the cattle industry.

Cohen, D. L. "The Botswana Political Elite: Evidence from the 1974 General Election." *Journal of Southern African Affairs* 4 (1979):347–370.

Description and analysis of the socioeconomic and political backgrounds of local and national candidates.

Cooper, David. "The State, Mineworkers, and Multinationals: The Selebi-Phikwe Strike, Botswana, 1975." In Gutkind, P.C.W.; Cohen, Robin; and Copans, Jean, eds., *African Labor History*, pp. 244–277. Beverley Hills, Calif.: Sage Publications, 1978.

Analysis of the consequences of a mineral-led development strategy through a description of mineworkers, the strike, and the government's responses.

_____ . "An Interpretation of the Emergent Urban Class Structure in Botswana: A Case Study of Selebi-Phikwe Miners." Ph.D. thesis, University of Birmingham, 1982.

A thorough study of class formation and changes connected with multinational mining corporations in partnership with the Botswanan government.

Holm, John. "Rural Development and Liberal Democracy in Botswana." *African Studies Review* 25:1 (March 1982):83–102.

A review of aspects of rural change and an analysis of obstacles to the political mobilization of the rural poor.

Jones, David. *Aid and Development in Southern Africa.* London: Croom Helm in association with Overseas Development Institute, 1977.

Compilation of material and commentary on foreign aid with a case study on Botswana.

Landell-Mills, P. M. "The 1969 Southern African Customs Union Agreement." *Journal of Modern African Studies* 9:2 (1971):263–282.

Surveys provisions of the agreement and its impact on revenue and development policy.

Parson, Jack. "Political Culture in Rural Botswana: A Survey Result." *Journal of Modern African Studies* 15 (1977):639–650.

Results of a 1974 survey of rural households relating political attitudes to the socioeconomic position of households.

_____ . "Cattle, Class, and the State in Rural Botswana." *Journal of Southern African Studies* 7:2 (April 1981):236–255.

Analysis of tribal grazing lands policy in terms of class composition of rural society and national government policymaking.

_____ . "The Trajectory of Class and State in Dependent Development: The Consequences of New Wealth for Botswana." *Journal of Commonwealth and Comparative Politics* 21:3 (1983):265–286.

Survey and analysis of class formation and politics in the postcolonial period.

Picard, Louis. "District Councils in Botswana: A Remnant of Local Autonomy." *Journal of Modern African Studies* 17 (1979):285–308.

Description and analysis of political decentralization in the independence era.

Werbner, Richard. "Small Man Politics and the Rule of Law: Centre-Periphery Relations in East-Central Botswana." *Journal of African Law* 21 (1977):24–39.

Microlevel study of local politics in the early independence period.

INTERNATIONAL RELATIONS

Carter, Gwendolen, and Morgan, E. Phillip, eds., *From the Front Line: Speeches of Sir Seretse Khama*. London: Rex Collings, 1980.
> Somewhat unevenly edited but a useful compilation concentrating on Botswana's international position and covering the independence period to about 1980.

Dale, Richard. "Botswana." In Potholm, Christian P., and Dale, Richard, eds., *Southern Africa in Perspective: Essays in Regional Politics*, pp. 110–124. New York: Free Press, 1972.
> Discussion of the parameters of Botswana's international position and the foundations of its foreign policy.

Thompson, Carol. *The Frontline States in the Liberation of Zimbabwe*. Boulder, Colo.: Westview Press, forthcoming.
> Excellent analysis of the southern African region in the world context. Chapters on Botswana and the Southern African Development Coordination Conference highlight the international position of Botswana.

Index

AAC. *See* Anglo American
    Corporation
Accelerated Rural Development
    Programme (1974), 51, 88–89,
    126(n33)
Act of Union (1910), 30
African American Labor Center, 94
African National Congress (ANC),
    110, 111, 112, 134(n36)
Afrikaners, 19, 20, 23, 102
Agricultural economy. *See* Economy,
    agricultural
Agricultural labor. *See* Labor,
    agricultural
Agriculture, 3, 23, 24, 27, 51, 59,
    69, 72, 81, 84, 91, 95, 116–117
    arable vs. livestock, 68
    commercialization of, 33, 60, 66,
    89
    crop production, 4, 10, 16, 66, 98
    See also Economy, agriculture;
    Labor, agricultural
ALDP. *See* Arable lands
    development policy
Alverson, Hoyt, 35
AMAX. *See* American Metal Climax
American Metal Climax (AMAX),
    75, 76, 77
Amin, Samir, 18
ANC. *See* African National
    Congress
Anglo American Corporation
    (AAC), 75, 76, 77
Apartheid, 2, 29, 30, 104, 107, 108,
    114. *See also* Botswana,

nonracialism of; Racial
    discrimination
Arable lands development policy
    (ALDP), 98–99

Bakwena society, 17
Bamangwato Concessions Limited
    (BCL), 75
Bangwaketse society, 54
Bangweto society, 17, 18
Bantustans, 29
Basutoland. *See* Botswana, and
    Basutoland (now Lesotho)
BCL. *See* Bamangwato Concessions
    Limited
BDC. *See* Botswana Development
    Corporation
BDP. *See* Botswana Democratic
    party
Bechuanaland
    colonization of, 20, 21, 113–114
    dependence on South Africa, 33
    employment in, 24–25
    foreign policy of, 101–103
    and Great Britain, 19–22, 27–28,
    29–31, 33
    nationalism in, 26–31
    northern (now Botswana), 20
    origins of, 14, 19
    self-government of, 31
    underdevelopment of, 25–26,
    33–34
Beef industry. *See* Cattle
BEF. *See* Botswana Employers'
    Association
BFTU. *See* Botswana Federation of
    Trade Unions

BIP. *See* Botswana Independence
  party
BMC. *See* Botswana Meat
  Commission
BNF. *See* Botswana National Front
Botswana
  administrative system, 41–46
  airport, 81
  and Angola, 107, 109, 111
  army, 81
  arts and crafts, 37–38
  associations, 37
  and Basutoland (now Lesotho),
    29, 58, 103, 109, 111
  Christianity in, 38
  Constitution, 39
  diplomatic representation in, 104
  diversification of dependence,
    104–106, 112
  economic growth, 3–4, 11, 16, 55,
    80, 95, 115. *See also* Botswana,
    economic problems
  economic problems, 57, 58
  foreign policy, 3–4, 101–112. *See
    also* International relations
  geography, 4, 6
  geopolitical position, 2–3
  government, 11, 12–13, 43–46,
    73, 75, 81, 107. *See also*
    Botswana, political structures
  and Great Britain, 3, 73, 102,
    103, 105, 113
  gross domestic product (GDP), 3,
    58, 77, 80
  and liberation in southern Africa,
    106–111
  location. *See* Botswana,
    geopolitical position
  and Mozambique, 107, 111, 112
  and Namibia, 108, 110, 112
  nonracialism of, 1, 106, 116
  political structures, 11–13, 38–56
  and Rhodesia, 101, 102, 106, 107,
    108, 109, 110
  size, 2
  and South Africa, 2, 3, 37, 79,
    95, 101, 102, 103, 104–107,
    108, 109, 110, 111, 112. *See also*
    Economic dependence, on
    South Africa
  and Soviet Union, 110
  sports, 38

  and Swaziland, 29, 103, 109, 111
  and Tanzania, 109
  trade, 2, 58. *See also* Commerce;
    individual industries
  and United States, 103, 105
  water resources, 4, 6, 58, 60, 68,
    76, 80, 81, 88, 91
  and Zambia, 106, 108, 109
  and Zimbabwe, 108, 109, 110,
    111, 112
Botswana Agricultural Marketing
  Board, 8, 68
Botswana Christian Council, 38
Botswana Council of Churches, 38
Botswana Defence Force, 109
Botswana Democratic party (BDP),
  1, 12, 31–33, 38, 39, 47–52,
  53, 54, 55, 66, 99, 114
Botswana Development Corporation
  (BDC), 79, 105, 106
Botswana Employers' Federation
  (BEF), 12, 94
Botswana Federation of Trade
  Unions (BFTU), 94
Botswana Independence party (BIP),
  31, 53
Botswana Meat Commission (BMC),
  68, 80
Botswana National Front (BNF), 12,
  33, 53–54
Botswana Peoples' party (BPP), 31,
  32, 52–53, 90
Botswana Roan Selection Trust
  (BRST), 75, 76–77
Bourgeoisie. *See* Class structures,
  middle class
BPP. *See* Botswana Peoples' party
British High Commission
  Territories, 22, 27, 29, 30
British South Africa Company
  (BSAC), 20, 102
BRST. *See* Botswana Roan Selection
  Trust
BSAC. *See* British South Africa
  Company
Bureaucracy, 35, 42, 43, 90

Capitalism, x, 13, 96, 106
Cattle, 1, 11, 16–17, 21, 23,
  24(photo), 25, 33, 43, 44, 59,
  66, 68, 69, 70, 80, 84, 88, 91,

96, 103, 105, 116, 117. *See also* Cattleowners

Cattleowners, 16, 59, 60, 67, 68, 69, 70, 89, 90, 91, 96, 114, 115, 117

Central-local government relations, 43–46

Chieftainship Act (1965), 43

Civil servants, 92, 94, 97

Class conflicts, 90–91, 95, 99–100, 116–117

Class relations, 13, 53–54, 60, 99, 115, 118. *See also* Class conflicts

Class structures
  middle class, 88, 90, 95, 115, 116–117, 118
  peasantariat, 26, 27, 29, 31, 32, 34, 43, 50, 51, 54, 59, 60, 68, 71, 72–73, 88–89, 90, 91, 92–93, 94, 95, 97, 98–100, 113, 114, 115, 116, 117–118, 123(n26)
  peasantry, 18, 29, 34, 69, 113
  political elite, 12, 35, 49, 50–51, 52, 55, 56, 91, 92, 105, 115, 116
  ruling class, 16–17, 18
  in Tswana societies, 16–17
  See also Class conflicts; Class relations

Climate
  rainfall, 4, 6, 16
  and vegetation, 6

Colonialism, ix, 6, 18–26, 28, 35, 43, 60–61, 88, 102, 114. *See also* Bechuanaland, colonization of

Commerce, 116, 117

Communications, 6, 8, 80. *See also* Infrastructural development

Conservation of resources, 111

Consolidation, 91

Copper/nickel deposits, 62, 75, 76

Credit Sales to Natives Proclamation (1923), 23

Crops. *See* Agriculture, crop production

Currency, 105–106

Customs Union agreement (1910), 22

Dale, Richard, 104

De Beers Botswana Mining Company (Debswana), 78–79

De Beers Consolidated Mines Limited, 77, 78

Decentralization, 44

Decolonization, 29

Democracy. *See* Liberalism

Demographics. *See* Population

Department of External Affairs, 104

Department of Labor, 64

Development and independence, "maxims" of, 104

Development expenditures, external sources, 74(table). *See also* Domestic development expenditures

Development Plan (1979–1985), 73, 86

Diamonds, 3, 62, 63, 77–78, 80, 81, 115

Difaqane, 18

District councils, power of, 43–44

Domestic development expenditures, 72, 80–81, 82–83(table), 84(table), 85

Drought, 6, 11, 60

Economic dependence
  on Great Britain, 58
  on South Africa, 1, 4, 22, 104–105, 109, 111

Economy
  agricultural, 6
  market, 111
  mineral-led, 62–65, 75–79, 80, 88, 90, 95, 115
  political. *See* Political economy
  rural, 6, 58, 65, 89, 97
  See also Botswana, economic growth; Botswana, economic problems; Exports; Imports; Infrastructural development; Labor reserve economy

Education, 6, 8, 28, 40, 42, 43, 58, 60, 68, 80, 81, 89. *See also* Infrastructural development; Schools

EEC. *See* European Economic Community

Elections, 1, 38, 43, 47, 48(table), 49, 50, 52, 54, 94, 115

Electricity, development of, 8, 58, 76
Elite, political. *See* Class structures, political elite
Employment
    public sector, 41–42, 87, 89
    in rural industries, 65, 69, 97
    and standard of living, 11, 64
    wage, 8, 23, 24, 25, 27, 58, 80, 88–89, 91, 95, 96, 117, 118
    See also Labor; Unemployment
Energy. *See* Electricity, development of; Infrastrutural development
Equality. *See* Liberalism
Ethnic groups, 35, 37, 43
European Economic Community (EEC), 103–104
Expatriates, European, 37, 42–43, 90
Expenditures, domestic development. *See* Domestic development expenditures
Expenditures, recurrent. *See* Recurrent expenditures
Exports, 1, 58, 80, 88, 96

Factories, 3
Farming. *See* Agriculture, crop production
Financial assistance policy (1982), 98
Foreign aid, 4, 104, 112
Foreign investment. *See* Investment, foreign
Free market, 105
Frontline States organization, 101, 109

Gaseitsiwe, Chief Bathoen, 33, 54
GDP. *See* Botswana, gross domestic product
Gold, 19, 89
Governing class, unity of, 115–116
Government. *See* Botswana, government
Government investment. *See* Investment, government
Grazing land, 4, 66, 68–69, 98. *See also* Overgrazing
Great Britain. *See* Botswana, and Great Britain

Health care, 68, 80, 88, 115. *See also* Infrastructural development
Hermans, H.C.L., 3
Hierarchy, tribal. *See* Tribal hierarchy
High Commission Territories. *See* British High Commission Territories
High Court, 12, 40
History
    colonial period, ix, 6, 18–26, 35, 43, 60–61, 88
    independence, 29–33. *See also* Independence, political
    precolonial period, 15–18
Holm, John, 50
House of Chiefs, 12, 40
Housing, 80, 98

Illiteracy, 27
"Imperial reserve," 21
Imports, 3, 9, 23
Import substitution, 80, 98
Income distribution, ix, 1, 4, 11, 89, 90, 92, 93(table), 94, 97, 115
Incorporation, territorial, 22, 27–28, 30
Indebtedness, loan, 76–77
Independence, political, 39, 41, 52, 57, 60, 61, 80, 101, 103, 106, 114. *See also* Self-government
Industry. *See* Cattle; Manufacturing industry; Mining industry
Inflation, 11, 81
Infrastructural development, 6, 7, 42, 55, 59, 60, 61, 72, 75–76, 80–81, 82–83(table), 84–85, 87–88, 91, 95, 96, 97, 114, 115, 116
Interbureau relations, 46
International aid. *See* Foreign aid
International relations, 103–104, 111–112
    and domestic development, 111
    See also Botswana, foreign policy
Investment
    foreign, 12, 63–64, 70, 72, 73, 74(table), 75, 79–80, 104, 105, 115
    government, 63–65, 72
    mining, 78–79, 115

Jameson, Leander, 20

Jobs. *See* Employment; Labor
Jwaneng mine, 77, 78, 79, 84

Kalahari Desert, 4
Kalanga people, 37, 52
Kaunda, Kenneth, 108
Kgalagadi Brewery, 80
Kgotla, 16, 17(photo), 41, 43
Khama, Ian, 99
Khama, Seretse, 2–3, 6, 31, 32,
    55–56, 66, 104–105, 106, 107,
    108, 109, 114
  death of, 47, 95
  marriage to Ruth Williams, 29–30
Kingship, in Tswana societies, 16,
    17
Koma, Kenneth, 33, 53–54

Labor
  agricultural, 3, 8, 23, 24, 25–26,
    27, 33, 69, 116, 117
  migratory, 10, 11, 23, 24–25, 26,
    27, 34, 57–59, 89, 95–96, 111,
    113, 115, 120(n9)
  See also Employment; Unions,
    trade; *individual industries*
Labor reserve economy, 33–34, 57,
    93, 102, 113
Land allocation, 43, 44, 67, 92, 98
"Land grab," 98
Land ownership, 8, 16, 66, 68, 91
Land rights, 91, 117
Land tenure, 60, 65–66, 68
Land use, 8, 65, 91–92
Lesotho. *See* Botswana, and
    Basutoland (now Lesotho)
Letlhakana mine, 77
Liberalism, 106, 133(n18)
Lipton, Michael, 95–96, 97
Livestock. *See* Agriculture, arable
    vs. livestock; Cattle; Oxen
Local Government Act, 44
Localization, administrative, 42–43
Lusaka Manifesto (1969), 109

Mafisa, 68
Majority rule, 106, 111, 112
Manufacturing industry, 3, 9, 58,
    66, 70, 72, 80, 96–97, 113, 116
Market economy. *See* Economy,
    market
Marx, Karl, x

Masire, Quett, 54, 55–56, 99
Matante, P. G., 31, 52
MFDP. *See* Ministry of Finance and
    Development Planning
Middle class. *See* Class structures,
    middle class
Migration, Tswana, 15
Migratory labor. *See* Labor,
    migratory
Mineral-led economy. *See* Economy,
    mineral-led
Minerals, 8–9, 19, 62, 69, 70. *See
    also* Copper/nickel deposits;
    Diamonds; Economy, mineral-
    led; Gold; Mining industry
Minimum wage(s), 64, 65, 89,
    92–93, 96
Mining industry, 1, 8–9, 12, 19, 23,
    24, 25, 27, 33, 58, 62, 66, 70,
    77, 87, 88, 95, 96, 99, 106,
    113, 116, 117
Mining investment. *See* Investment,
    mining
Ministry of Commerce and
    Industry, 64
Ministry of Finance and
    Development Planning (MFDP),
    73
Ministry of Local Government and
    Lands (MLGL), 12, 44, 46
Ministry of Works and
    Communications, 72
Missionaries, 19, 20, 38
MLGL. *See* Ministry of Local
    Government and Lands
Mogwe, A. M., 103
Mozambique. *See* Botswana, and
    Mozambique
Mpho, Motsamai, 31, 53

Namibia. *See* Botswana, and
    Namibia; South West Africa
National Assembly, 12, 38–40, 107,
    124(n2), 125(n9)
National Employment, Manpower,
    and Incomes Council (NEMIC),
    64
Nationalism, 28, 114
National party, 29
National Policy on Tribal Grazing
    Land (1975), 67

NEMIC. *See* National Employment, Manpower, and Incomes Council
Nonalignment policy, 107
Noninterference policy, 107
Nyerere, Julius, 109

OAU. *See* Organization of African Unity
Okavango River, 4
Oppenheimer, Harry F., 77
Opposition parties. *See* Botswana Independence party; Botswana National Front; Botswana Peoples' party
Orapa mine, 77, 78
Organization of African Unity (OAU), 103, 107, 109
"Outward reach" policy, 107
Overgrazing, 8, 66, 67, 70, 91
Oxen, 59, 68, 89

"Paper citizens," 37
"Parallel rule," 21
Parliament, 12, 38, 39, 40, 49, 50
Peasantariat. *See* Class structures, peasantariat
Peasantry. *See* Class structures, peasantry
Peoples' Republic of China (PRC), 110
Pim Report, 27
Political economy, x, 57, 87–88, 113, 117
    definition of, 13
Population
    distribution, 6, 9–11, 58
    growth, 10
    origins of, 15
    size, 2, 66, 121(n31)
Poverty, 11, 28, 89. *See also* Botswana, economic problems
Power supplies, 6. *See also* Electricity, development of
PRC. *See* Peoples' Republic of China
Precolonial period. *See* History, precolonial period
Preindependence. *See* Colonialism
Presidential Commission on Local Government Structure (1979), 45

Quality of life. *See* Employment, and standard of living

Racial discrimination, 28, 106, 108
Railway, 21, 81, 102
Rainfall. *See* Climate, rainfall
Rand Monetary Area, 58
Recurrent expenditures, 86–87
Refugees, 37, 107, 110
Resource allocations, 72–73, 75, 80–85, 90, 95, 96
Rhodes, Cecil, 19, 20
Rhodesia. *See* Botswana, and Rhodesia
Rhodesia Railways, 105, 110
Rinderpest epidemic, 21, 23
Roads, development of, 6, 7, 8, 57–58, 69, 76, 80, 81, 85, 86, 88, 105, 114, 115, 116. *See also* Infrastructural development
Ruling class. *See* Class structures, ruling class
Rural development, 4, 65–70, 81, 84
    program, goals of, 65, 66
    See also Economy, rural
Rural economy. *See* Economy, rural

SADCC. *See* Southern African Development Coordination Conference
Salariat, 89, 130(n36)
Salaries Review Commission (1980), 97
Savanna, 4, 6, 7(map)
Schapera, I., 27, 28, 29
Schools, 6, 8, 81, 85, 88, 89, 114, 115, 116. *See also* Education
Seboni, W., 54
Sehuba, 17
Selebi-Phikwe mine, 75, 76, 94
Self-government, 30–31
Self-sufficiency
    budgetary, 21, 61–62, 103
    of peasantariat, 89, 96, 113
Shashe Project, 75
South Africa, 9, 21, 29, 57, 58, 60, 114, 117
    Afrikaners in, 19, 20, 23
    British interests in, 19, 22, 30
    forced migration in, 18
    foreign workers in, 24–25

See also Botswana, and South
    Africa
Southern African Customs Union,
    3, 58, 80, 109
    Agreement, 61
Southern African Development
    Coordination Conference
    (SADCC), 4, 101, 109
South West Africa, 106
South West Africa Peoples'
    Organization (SWAPO), 112
Soviet Union. *See* Botswana, and
    Soviet Union
Soweto uprising, 108, 110
Standard of living. *See*
    Employment, and standard of
    living
Strikes, 93, 94
SWAPO. *See* South West Africa
    Peoples' Organization
Swaziland. *See* Botswana, and
    Swaziland

Tanzania. *See* Botswana, and
    Tanzania
Taxation, 21, 22–23, 25, 40, 44, 64,
    65, 113
TGLP. *See* Tribal grazing lands
    policy
Tiro, Abraham, 110
Trade. *See* Botswana, trade
Trade union law, 94
Trading Act, 45
*Transitional Plan for Social and
    Economic Development*, 61
Transportation system, 81, 85, 98.
    See also Infrastructural
    development; Railway; Roads,
    development of
Tribal grazing lands policy (TGLP),
    67, 68, 69, 70, 81, 91, 92, 98
Tribal hierarchy, 16–17, 18, 34

Tribal Land Boards, 67–68
"Tributary social formations," 18
Tswana societies, 15–19, 20, 35, 52,
    101–102, 122(n3)

Underdevelopment, 25–26, 27, 33,
    58, 59, 60, 101, 104
Unemployment, 69, 96
Unified Local Government Service,
    46
Unions
    customs, 9, 88, 102
    trade, 12, 72, 94, 95
United Nations, 103, 107, 109
    Committee on Colonialism, 31
United States. *See* Botswana, and
    United States
Urbanization, 10

Vegetation, 4, 7(map). *See also*
    Climate, and vegetation;
    Savanna
Veterinary projects, 61

Wage employment. *See*
    Employment, wage
Wagon trade, 18
Water rights, 66–67, 91
Williams, Ruth, 29–30
Women
    and agriculture, 10, 16, 26, 59,
    114
    and child care, 16
    and family management, 114
    and upkeep of household, 26
Working class. *See* Class structures,
    peasantariat

Zambezi River, 4
Zambia. *See* Botswana, and Zambia
Zimbabwe. *See* Botswana, and
    Zimbabwe
Zoning. *See* Land allocation